Greenhead Politics

Greenhead Politics

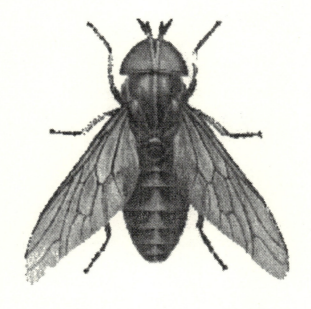

✦

The Story Brigantine Taxpayers Were Never Told

Patrick Costello

iUniverse, Inc.
New York Lincoln Shanghai

Greenhead Politics
The Story Brigantine Taxpayers Were Never Told

iUniverse books may be ordered through booksellers or by contacting:

iUniverse
2021 Pine Lake Road, Suite 100
Lincoln, NE 68512
www.iuniverse.com
1-800-Authors (1-800-288-4677)

The following story is based on true events. Certain names and events have been changed. All quotations in italics are taken from legal documents or news reports.

ISBN-13: 978-0-595-36763-4 (pbk)
ISBN-13: 978-0-595-81182-3 (ebk)
ISBN-10: 0-595-36763-1 (pbk)
ISBN-10: 0-595-81182-5 (ebk)

Printed in the United States of America

Contents

MAP OF BRIGANTINE

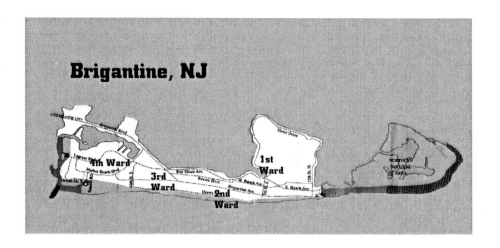

AUTHOR'S NOTE:

The following story is based on true events. Certain names and events have been changed. All quotations in italics are taken from legal documents or news reports.

Prologue

The story of the murder-suicide spreads through the small island community with the speed of a brush fire. It is not often that the local gossip mill has such juicy material in which to sink its teeth, and opportunities like this are not to be squandered. Shocking enough on its own, what with revelations of scandal, murder and suicide in a well-known local family, the tale is made even more attractive by the rumblings of a political element that promises to rock the very foundations of the city itself.

All over town, televisions are tuned to TV40, the local news station; in anticipation of the bomb that those in the know insist will soon be dropped. In a local tavern, a group of city employees hunches forward over their beers and asks the bartender to turn up the sound on the TV. At the home of the Mayor, a group of City Council members sits in stunned disbelief and dread of whatever further problems the broadcast might bring down upon their already troubled heads. On the other end of town, a smaller group of Council members, accompanied by a few political acolytes, rubs their hands together in anticipation of the destruction of a formidable enemy. And in one home, tucked away on a quiet street bordering the golf course, one man sits alone in front of his television and watches in disbelief as his life is turned upside down.

The bleach-blonde newscaster stares directly into the camera and smiles vacantly. Sporting the same vacant gleam in her eye, the same cheerful tone with which she would introduce a story about fuzzy kitties up for adoption, she begins reading from the teleprompter. *"The union representing Brigantine's Public Works employees is calling on the Director of that department to resign. As Kara Silver reports, many local members blame alleged harassment by the Director as playing a part in yesterday's murder-suicide in nearby Egg Harbor Township."* With that, the news anchor hands the story off to her reporter and promptly forgets about it as her hair and makeup are fixed in preparation for her next report.

The camera cuts to another pretty, blonde-haired woman with a microphone, standing outside of what appears to be some sort of municipal building. She

1

begins her fateful report. *"More than two dozen grief-stricken Brigantine Public Works employees met behind closed doors today with a crisis intervention counselor."*

The picture dissolves to a close-up shot of a sad-looking city worker heaving a heavy sigh and turning to dejectedly walk away from the camera, as the reporter's voice-over intones, *"They're dealing with the loss of co-worker Joe Manera, a thirty-year veteran of the Public Works Department. Prosecutors say Manera shot his wife to death yesterday and turned the gun on himself. Many of Manera's co-workers say they can't presume to know what would make one take a life, but they say stress on the job was likely a factor."*

The camera shot switches to a close up of an angry-looking city employee, who states, *"I'm not saying it's the only circumstance that led to this, but it definitely did contribute heavily."*

Kara Silver comes back on-screen, *"Most of the workers believe years of alleged harassment by their boss, Public Works Director John Costello, proved too much for Manera to handle."*

The shot again quickly changes to another close-up, this time of a bereaved union representative, who says, *"The Union would request at this time that he would resign. The things that transpired in the last few days demonstrate the type of stress that is put on individuals that work in this department."*

Another quick cut back to our intrepid reporter. *"Nearly a dozen different grievances have been filed against Costello, but representatives of Teamsters local 331 say the city has turned a blind eye to the problem because of Costello's political connections."*

With the sound bites flying fast and furious, our view changes to a close-up of another city employee, who angrily claims, *"Joe had talked to every council member and to the Mayor, begging them to please do something."*

We quickly bounce back to a full view of the reporter, standing in front of the city building once again. With evident disbelief in her words, she says, *"Although Joe Manera had filed a harassment grievance with his union and against the city's Director of Public Works, the Public Works Director denies ever knowing about that grievance or even ever having a problem with Mr. Manera at all."*

The shot cuts to a close-up of John Costello, the Director in question, who seems bewildered and caught off-guard. He says, *"This has just been tragic. We're all in shock. I never had a problem with Joe. My sympathy goes out to the families."* In true television tradition, much more time is devoted to accusation and innuendo that to any response. Costello's denial seems perfunctory at best, or at least edited to appear so.

As if to refute Costello's claims, the reporter wraps up the story with her solemn final words. *"Along with the union, the City Manager says Brigantine will address grievances from DPW more aggressively in the future. In Brigantine, this is Kara Silver, for NewsCenter 40."*

Thus ends the television news report. However, the story is far from over.

1

An Island You'll Love For Life

Less than a mile away from the bright lights and clanging bells of Atlantic City sits the idyllic island community of Brigantine, New Jersey. First observed in 1608 by explorer Henry Hudson, Brigantine was named for the type of sailing ship that was most often found wrecked in the dangerous offshore shoals of the island. In the days of canvas and wood, the area was well known and feared by every ship's captain who sailed the Atlantic coast. Since the early 1700's, more than 300 vessels have been wrecked off the shore of Brigantine, and with the right tide, a few carcasses of more modern victims can still be seen out past the breakers.

But the offshore shoals were not the only danger lurking around this peaceful-seeming little island. Adding to the romance of the shipwrecks is the lore of pirates. Legendary pirates Captain Kidd and Blackbeard are reputed to have buried treasure under the sand of Brigantine beaches, and while historical accounts of those times are sketchy at best, there is reason to believe that both men at least frequented the area, although no treasure has been discovered to date. With two inlets alongside the main shipping route, one appropriately named "Wreck Inlet", Brigantine was an excellent hideout for pirates, both as a repository for treasure and as a staging point for attacks on unwary ships. While a poor, beleaguered captain was occupied guiding his ship through the treacherous offshore waters, he also had to be mindful of the possibility that at any moment, pirates could streak out of one of the inlets and be upon him before he knew it.

Indeed, so strategically placed for such maneuvers was Brigantine that the same methods were adopted by American privateers during the Revolutionary War. More than a few incautious or disabled British ships were ambushed and sent to the bottom by American ships hiding in ambush in a Brigantine inlet. Whalers also found the island useful as a staging area to launch attacks on migrating pods of whales leaving the coast of New England for warm southern waters. Today the island atones for this by hosting the Marine Mammal Stranding Center, which assists sick and injured whales, dolphins, seals and other marine life in peril. In fact, half of Brigantine's 6.39 square miles of area is owned by the State of New Jersey under the Green Acres Program, and serves as a protected wildlife sanctuary.

Throughout its long history, several attempts have been made to develop Brigantine on a more significant scale, even going so far as to change the name of the town to North Atlantic City. It was in this same period, the late 1880's, that a railroad was built connecting Brigantine to the comparatively thriving metropolis of Philadelphia. During the 1890's, sixteen trolleys ran the length of the island and steamboats ferried passengers across the inlet to Atlantic City and back. A few hotels opened, and Brigantine started to gain its own identity as a vacation hideaway, even hosting such notables as President Grover Cleveland. However, the realities of surviving as a seasonal resort town were too much for the burgeoning community, and hard times, as well as harsh weather, ended their boom in the early 1900's. By 1917, Brigantine had only 54 full-time residents and an operating budget of just over five thousand dollars.

During the 1920's, ninety percent of the land in Brigantine was acquired by an incorporation of wealthy Atlantic City businessmen and brokers known as the Island Development Company, which immediately proceeded to undertake serious development of the community. This entailed not only the construction of a bridge linking the island to Atlantic City, but also a school, church, streets, sidewalks, bulkheads and jetties. The Island Development Company was also instrumental in the construction of several hundred homes, a one-mile long boardwalk, a 500-foot pier and a modern hotel. This was in addition to an 18-hole golf course, which attracted many of the pro golfers of the period. Automobile access to the island instigated a rise in the value and desirability of owning land on the small island getaway, and suddenly, Brigantine was a city on the rise.

In 1926, the Brigantine Lighthouse, which to many has become the symbol of Brigantine, was built. Ironically, this was not a reaction to the infamy of Brigantine as a dangerous area for shipping and sailing, but rather as a landmark and tourist attraction. During the Depression, it even served as the headquarters for the Brigantine Police. However, much to the chagrin of hundreds of ship's captains, at no time did it ever serve in the traditional capacity of a lighthouse.

At the same time, the city was also creating the vital infrastructure necessary for a permanent community. Sewer lines had to be dug, as well as a water supply established. Twenty miles of streets had to be created and paved. To raise the required funds for such an undertaking, the city of Brigantine sold municipal bonds. However, the stock market crash of 1929 rendered those bonds worthless as the boom ended and the Great Depression began. With no more demand for land, the Island Development Company went under and deeded its remaining properties to the city.

During World War 2, the US Army's Coastal Warning Service was seeking a place to use as an observation point to watch out for invasion by sea. The beachfront location of the Brigantine Inn, combined with the fact that it was the tallest building in the area, made it a perfect choice. After surviving a devastating hurricane in 1944, which destroyed the only bridge off the island and forced residents to be ferried back and forth across the inlet to Atlantic City during the 21 months of repairs, Brigantine rebounded and began to grow steadily once again. The schools were expanded and businesses began to move into town to serve the residents. The postwar boom was good for Atlantic City, which was good for Brigantine's prospects for the future as a suburb to the resort community.

In 1975, entrepreneur Carmen Ricci presented the city with plan to remodel the old Seahorse Pier at the north end of Brigantine into an amusement pier, which would attract some tourism of its own to Brigantine. He built the Brigantine Castle, which held the dubious distinction of being the largest freestanding wood structure in the United States.

The Brigantine Castle, which burned down in 1987, is remembered by locals and visitors as an all-time great haunted house attraction.

The Brigantine Castle haunted house and amusement pier opened in the summer of 1976 to huge success. To this day, it is remembered as one of the premier haunted house attractions ever. In fact, it was too successful for many Brigantine residents' liking. Due to a larger than usual advertising campaign, the Castle was drawing over a million tourists annually from along the east coast, despite only being open from May to September. This resulted in many problems for residents in the vicinity of the pier, which combined with the huge increase in traffic and parking problems among others, made the attraction none too popular with the city in which it resided. The infrastructure of the quiet little community was simply not equipped to handle the results of such a popular tourist attraction, and the locals began to resent the intrusion. Subsequently, the city adopted a few ordinances which hurt the Castle's business, and when that didn't get the message across, the city took advantage of the hysteria resulting after a fire in the haunted house at Great Adventure and launched an investigation into the safety of the Castle's structure. It was basically a fishing expedition, and it was successful. Structural problems were discovered in the pier itself, and rather than fight any longer, Ricci closed it down in 1984. He sold the property in 1987, and ironically, the week that demolition was to take place, the Castle burnt to the ground. Rumors flew about a supposed "insurance job", but the blaze was reportedly set by local teens, who used the abandoned structure as a hangout.

Aside from the Brigantine Castle, the second most notorious feature of the island was as a spawning ground for the Greenhead, or *Tabanus nigrovittatus,* a particularly vicious and insidious species of horsefly that breeds in the surrounding marshlands. Indigenous to most of southern New Jersey, the Greenhead nevertheless seems to have a special affinity for the island of Brigantine, which is known locally as "The Greenhead capital of the world." Because they occur in large numbers, have a long flight range, and attack persistently, they pose a problem for beachgoers throughout the summer months. Larger than most common horseflies, and much more intelligent, the reputation of the Greenhead among those who have suffered its wraith is frightful. Possessed of an almost evil cunning, the Greenhead will wait until its victim is most vulnerable, such as when laden with groceries or small children, and will then attack relentlessly. For Brigantine residents, the sight of an out-of-towner, or "shoobie" as locals refer to tourists, maniacally jumping about and swatting at his legs, is as common on the beach as lifeguards and bikinis.

However, what had to be the biggest determining factor in the shaping of the destiny of Brigantine was the 1978 legalization of casino gambling in Atlantic City. The face of Atlantic City, and with it the fortune of Brigantine, was changed forever. The World's Playground was back as a major east coast tourist destination, and the little island next door was reaping all the attending benefits. To an area with a high percentage of blue-collar tradesmen, the building boom that came along with the advent of the casinos was a godsend. The strength of the flagging local trade unions was suddenly increased exponentially, and the standard of living of their members rose sharply.

Besides the local residents who made their livings building the actual structures, the arrival of the casinos also provided a stable job base for the area. Thousands of well-paying positions needed to be filled right away, and people who previously did not really have much in the way of prospects were now finding themselves with decent jobs. The sudden influx of money into the area brought on an unprecedented period of prosperity from which Brigantine could not help but benefit. Thousands of new casino employees would soon be moving into the area, and where better to house them than the nice little island right next door, just sitting there waiting to be developed?

Relatively empty, at least from a modern standpoint, Brigantine was wide open for the building boom. Entire housing developments sprang up virtually overnight, and in all income ranges, with little thought given to aesthetics or layout. This has resulted in the south end of the island containing multi-million dollar bay-front mansions and low-income housing projects within the same square mile. It also resulted in greatly increased wealth for those who had positioned themselves to benefit from the boom, such as property speculators and building contractors. Of course, the writing had been on the wall for years previous that legalized gambling was on the way, and more than a few shrewd investors managed to grab up a significant amount of land in anticipation of just such a development.

As far as the political spectrum, until 1989 Brigantine operated under the Commission form of government, with an elected three-person commission, which themselves picked a figurehead Mayor, with no veto power, to "preside" over them. However, beyond the official local government, Brigantine has, in recent generations, served as something of an unofficial county seat, as well.

The name Frank S. Farley is familiar to New Jersey residents, if for no other reason, than simply because so many public areas bear his name. Having served as state Senator for over thirty years, "Hap" Farley was a huge player in the Republican machine that ran the area's politics and society. His base of power was Atlantic County, and in particular, the Atlantic City area. One of his staunchest local political allies was Vincent Haneman, a Brigantine resident and future Associate Justice of the State Supreme Court, after whom the modern Brigantine Bridge is named.

Haneman was vigorously active in city politics, serving as mayor of Brigantine for eight years, President of the Chamber of Commerce, president of the board of education, and even as a representative in the state assembly. After his death in

1978, his son, Howard, "Fritz" Haneman carried on the family name in local politics. Fritz had served in the SAS, which was the precursor to the CIA, so while he certainly aspired to political power like that of his father, he had been educated to assume somewhat lower of a profile. He did not hold nearly as many official positions as his father had, but he successfully established himself as a major political mover and shaker in Atlantic County. Every state politician has his "guy who gets things done" on the local level and for Farley, Fritz Haneman was that guy.

As head of the Republican Party for the area, Fritz made Brigantine the county seat simply by virtue of living there. All the big political names made sure when they passed through to make a stop in Brigantine to see Fritz Haneman and pay respects. In addition, for anyone aspiring to be elected to any position of significance, the Haneman stamp of approval was mandatory. When a potential candidate made the rounds among the established politicos, trying to gather support for his ambitions, it was a well-known fact in insider circles that Fritz would signal his choice by accompanying his candidate to the meeting. No other aspirants were even taken seriously. By way of example of Haneman's power, it is a little-known fact that because of his efforts, Brigantine was actually considered as a possible site for the United Nations building, which was eventually built in New York City.

As high-powered as he was on the county and state level, Fritz Haneman stayed very much in the game at a local level as well. Such was the power of the Republican Party in Brigantine that until recently it was unheard of for any sane resident to be a declared Democrat. To be so was to be ostracized, and rendered ineligible for any of the wide variety of patronage available to those who demonstrated political loyalty. If you wanted to be a police officer or a fire fighter, there was a certain route to be taken, and the higher the political activity of your family, the better your chances. Membership in the Republican Club was a must. Requiring less, but still substantial political support were the lifeguard and public works positions. Alternatively, maybe you just wanted a streetlight on your corner, so your children would not have to wait for the school bus in the dark. No problem, as long as you knew how to play the game. Whatever the case, if you needed it done in Brigantine, Fritz Haneman was the man to see.

However, you would not know it to look at him. Very much a common man, or at least wishing to appear so, Fritz favored paint-spattered work pants and baseball caps over what might be considered more suitable attire for a man of his means. He kept most of his political meetings very informal, and did more business in his garage, or in the stands at the baseball field, than he ever did at Republican Club headquarters. To casual observers, Fritz drove the same old blue Suburban year after year. In reality, he purposefully bought the exact same vehicle every few years, so as never to give any public indications of his status.

As the head of the Republican Party, and the only game in town, Fritz was always on the lookout for a new candidate on the rise, and he found one in Emmitt Turner, a schoolteacher turned newspaper publisher. Turner was a longtime Brigantine resident who had enough intelligence and personable charm to be politically useful to the Republican Party, and he was heavily courted as Haneman's next fair-haired boy. While most assumed Turner was destined to be the next Mayor of Brigantine, the plan was actually to bypass city politics altogether and seek election of Turner as County Freeholder. Fritz had great things planned for his new star player.

Unfortunately, the harsh glare of the spotlight was a bit too much for Turner to withstand. There were whispers about his personal life, which, under normal circumstances, would have been considered nothing more than idle gossip. However, as is true in all levels of politics, once one's hat has been thrown into the political ring, nothing is off limits. The most insignificant personal indiscretion can become fodder for one's opponents to a ridiculous degree, which is a fact of political life that can frighten away even the most sincerely motivated potential candidate. Of course, none of this gossip was ever investigated or even officially alleged, which is of small consolation once the damage has been done. True or not, these rumors served to torpedo Turner's promising political career before it ever had a chance to set sail. For public consumption, the story was simply that Turner did not have the desire or dedication it took to run for high office. He was replaced by a young man named Kurt Conover, who went on to hold the post of Chairman of the Atlantic County Board of Freeholders, and now serves as State Assemblyman.

It is not clear whether righteous indignation or sour grapes were his motivation, but Turner's fall from grace ignited his revolutionary fires, and he responded with a crusade to change the landscape of Brigantine politics. Turner had been privy to high-level information in the Republican Club, and he knew where many bodies were buried, an advantage which he exploited at every opportunity. He found financial backing in local developer and entrepreneur Bill Miller, and together they purchased their own newspaper. Heretofore an innocuous little advertising circular, the Brigantine Beachcomber newspaper was transformed into a political forum for an attack on the status quo.

What Turner sought was no less than an entire change in the form of Brigantine's government. Instead of the Commission form of government, which had been in effect since 1931, Turner espoused the Council-Manager form under the Faulkner Act of New Jersey. Under Faulkner, their government would consist of a Mayor, two at-large Councilmen, four ward Councilmen, and a Council-appointed City Manager. Looking to break the Republican stranglehold on the island, Turner's strategy might have been to create as many elected positions as possible, thereby increasing the chance of partisan diversity.

Whatever his strategy, Turner certainly had the Republicans nervous. He was charismatic, and had gained popular support by doing a lot of grass-roots campaigning in the Brigantine taverns. He also had a formidable public platform in his own newspaper, which he used to air all of the Republican Club's dirty laundry in an effort to get enough voters angry enough at the present regime to vote for a new form of government out of sheer spite. Despite all the political maneuvering the present regime could muster, Turner managed to get the issue on the ballot in 1989. The result was a disaster for the Republican old guard. The measure passed by a mere 41 votes, and the status quo was knocked on its ear. The problem was not so much that the form of government would change. That was simply a change in the tune to which they all had to dance. The bigger issue was the fact that the upstart Turner had been successful in convincing the notoriously Republican voters to go against the established tradition of the last fifty years. That did not bode particularly well for the success of any potential Republican candidates in the coming City Council and Mayoral elections.

In addition to all these problems, the Republican machine was facing the loss of one its key components. Fritz Haneman was elderly and not in the best of health. He was looking to spend less time in meetings with politicians, and more time in meetings with his grandchildren. He was finished looking for new candidates to get elected. At his age, it was time to start looking for a successor. A new generation had taken over the reins of power in Brigantine, and Haneman knew that the Republican Club needed someone from that generation to step forward and lead the way in the new political climate. He even had someone in mind to take over his position as behind-the-scenes Godfather of the Republican Club when he retired. He had taken under his wing the son of some longtime friends, John and Josephine Costello, and young John was turning out to be a particularly apt pupil.

2

Welcome to the Machine

John Costello lived in Brigantine almost his entire life, and never really cared about politics. He was too busy earning a living.

Born in 1948, John Costello was the second of four children born to John and Josephine Costello, lifelong residents of the island. In a small island community like the Brigantine of the 1950's, childhood was all about summertime and getting in the water. Growing up in a bayside home on affluent West Shore Drive afforded all the swimming, clamming, crabbing and fishing opportunities one could ask for, with the bay only footsteps away. John enjoyed all the standard advantages of a suburban middle class upbringing, and was active in local sports and clubs.

An average student, John graduated from Atlantic City High School and briefly attended college before meeting and marrying Barbara Eby, a red-haired beauty from nearby Hammonton. Shortly after, he was accepted into the apprenticeship program for the electrical union. The International Brotherhood of Electrical Workers, or the IBEW, provided quality on-the-job training and promised a man a decent living wage, but for a first-year apprentice, the pay simply was not enough to support a family. Therefore, when the couple's first child came in 1968, John was working two or even three different jobs at once. The construction industry was slow, and for a brief period in 1977, Costello was forced to pack up his family and move to Monaca, PA, a small steel town just outside of Pittsburgh. Through the union, members are permitted to travel to other areas and work in places where construction is heavy and extra electricians are needed, and the steel mills were hiring for long hours and big pay. Having had a second son in 1975, the young Costello family needed the money badly enough to load up and drive the eight hours to their temporary new home.

All that changed with the advent of casino gaming in Atlantic City. Now John's home local, IBEW Local 211, was suddenly booming, and it was time to move the family back home to Brigantine. The construction business exploded in Atlantic City, as formerly poor construction workers were suddenly making more money than they had ever made before in their lives. Now Atlantic City was the place to which the workers traveled from around the country. John emerged as one of the most respected members of his union, being chosen to serve as the general foreman on several huge projects, such as the Sands Casino, and the Trump Marina. He also operated his own electrical contracting company, having passed the stringent state testing requirements for not only an electrical contractor's license, but also being licensed as an inspector and sub-code official. With his success in the electrical industry, Costello was able to provide a comfortable life for his family, and he began to have the time to get more involved in his community.

John had known the Haneman family his whole life, as Fritz and John's father had been friends as far back as he could remember. He never really got too involved in politics, although he was certainly not naïve to the political realities of his hometown. He knew who really ran Brigantine. So when he saw the things that Emmitt Turner was printing in the Beachcomber, it was only natural that he give Fritz Haneman a call to ask what was going on and offer assistance. To his surprise, Costello found himself invited to an informal gathering that very evening at Haneman's luxurious bay-front home. He was flattered to be granted such easy access, and saw an opportunity to play a role in shaping his community for the better. Haneman's motivations, however, were not so benign, at least at first. For while he certainly recognized the value in another young, enthusiastic, upwardly-mobile ally, Haneman also sought to obtain from Costello the politically valuable membership list of the electrician's union. Although he failed with regard to his ulterior motives, Haneman discovered that the decision to extend the invitation was bearing fruit after all. John Costello had turned out to be quite politically astute, and to his unexpected delight, Fritz had found himself a new protégé.

Through Haneman, Costello was granted entrance to the inside world of politics, a world of influence and patronage, of respect and privilege. He suddenly found himself rubbing elbows with Senators and Assemblymen, but even more influential to him were the national-level political players. Haneman introduced John to people who had run campaigns for some big name politicians, and their lessons were not lost on him. Costello was turning out to be pretty good at the political game, if a little heavy-handed at times, and Fritz felt better having such a loose cannon under control and on his side. Whereas Haneman navigated the political waters gently and with a certain understated grace, Costello came to be regarded as something of a shark, slashing his way through obstacles and exhibiting a take-no-prisoners style in his campaign strategies. However, with Emmitt Turner already successful at changing Brigantine's form of government and with the first elections under that new governance just around the corner, for the first time there was a real danger that the Republican grip on Brigantine might be slipping. The status quo was facing an unprecedented threat, and those in a position to lose power were highly in favor of a more aggressive political strategy. By January of 1992, John Costello was not only the President of the Brigantine Republican Club, but also served as Municipal Chairman of the Republican Party for Atlantic County.

John Costello, pictured with then-NJ Governor Christine Todd Whitman, at the Governor's residence at Drumthwacket, NJ.

Immediately upon taking the helm, Costello set the tone for the entire campaign by firing a shot directly across the enemy's bow. John put out the word, unofficially of course, that he was offering a reward for any juicy tidbit that might embarrass or otherwise discredit mayoral candidate Emmitt Turner. It turned out to be a brilliant strategy, distracting Turner from the election and keeping the Democrats off balance, always waiting for the other shoe to drop. Costello has never publicly commented on whether or not anyone ever collected the bounty.

Up for grabs in the election were several positions, and the Republican party intended to hang on to as many as possible. Besides the mayoral post, there were two at-large council seats and four ward council positions to be filled for the first time, and potential candidates were coming out of the woodwork. Every frustrated political firebrand saw in the newly created openings an opportunity to finally be heard in a previously closed arena.

Consequently, the scramble for party nominations was intense, and Costello had to be careful when deciding the Republican candidates. The wrong step would not only spell defeat, but also the end of his blossoming political career, which John was quite beginning to enjoy. When the smoke cleared, the Republicans had won in a rout. Turner had been beaten handily by Andrew Solari, a former county freeholder who, at the request of senior party officials, had resigned his county seat to run for Mayor of his hometown. Ed "Scoop" Kay and Phil Geunther had taken the At Large council seats, and Republican candidates won in three of the four wards. Only the fourth ward had fallen under Democratic control, and that was hardly a surprise since the winner, Joe Messick, was the most experienced political operator the Democrats had. Immediately, plans for the next election began to take shape, as the Republicans were not to be satisfied with anything less than total victory. According to the structure of the new government, the council and mayoral served four-year terms, with staggered elections. That meant it would only be two years before the Republicans had another shot at that fourth ward seat, and complete control of the island.

As it turned out, they were successful in ousting Messick, who lost to Mike Hilferty in the next election. Nevertheless, a funny thing happened to the Republicans on their way to total domination. They concentrated so hard on the fourth ward that the second and third slipped right through their fingers. Second ward Councilman Harrison Butler, a slick, young attorney who was seemingly named with a political career in mind, found himself embroiled in private financial difficulties that overshadowed his political concerns and precluded a second term. Butler was unseated by Democrat Phyllis Koch, whose main qualification for public office seemed to be her career as a gym teacher in the Brigantine school system. Fortunately, Koch proved unmemorable and was unseated easily in the following elections by Republican Richard Casamento.

The first ward Councilman, Robert Solari, was an Atlantic City firefighter and the brother of the mayor. He had no trouble retaining his post as representative of Brigantine's most Republican ward in subsequent elections, and holds the same Council seat to this day. Quite an accomplishment in a small town with such a turbulent political atmosphere, especially considering the fact that his private life has been a subject frequently on the lips of the town gossips. Whatever his personal peccadilloes, Solari has performed competently, if quietly, and retained his position for over ten years.

Republican Dan Dailey was taken by surprise and ousted in the third ward by Anne Phillips, who had earned a reputation as a staunch political activist, if a bit overzealous. Phillips had long acted as a self-appointed community watchdog, which did not do much to ingratiate her with the established political machine, but she had won support from the third ward residents through sheer tireless effort. The elderly Phillips attended council meetings obsessively, hounding the Council on seemingly every issue, and consistently spoke out on the need for accountability in government. Soon, her over-zealousness was rewarded when the Democrats recognized her for the untapped resource she was and recruited her to go after Dailey's Council seat.

Things got worse when fourth ward Councilman Mike Hilferty suddenly decided to step down. Hilferty was well liked and very competent by all accounts, but did not have the constitution for the constant turmoil and infighting of politics. Unable to separate his personal feelings from his political dealings, Hilferty's performance began to suffer because of the constant stress. The situation culminated when he almost came to blows with an irate resident at a Council meeting, in a very public spectacle that only worsened Hilferty's condition. Soon his health had deteriorated to the point that he had to be hospitalized for the effects of the stress, and he had no choice but to step down. Replacing Hilferty as fourth ward Councilman was Republican James Frugoli, a longtime resident with a newly acquired taste for political power. As if these problems were not enough, there were rumblings of discontent coming from the office of the Mayor himself. Andy Solari had been perfectly happy as a county freeholder, and had only reluctantly given up that post to run in Brigantine at the behest of state Senator Bill Gormley.

(L to R) 3rd Ward Councilman Sam Storino, 4th Ward Councilman James Frugoli, 2nd Ward Councilman Richard Casamento, 1st Ward Councilman Robert Solari

The Republicans had been shaken by Emmitt Turner's success in changing the form of government, and turned to the popular Andy Solari to ensure their continued control over the city's highest office. Solari had been assured by senior party officials that he was only needed to help fend off Turner, and that once the danger had passed he could return to his county freeholder position and a bright future. When this promise was broken and Solari's county seat was filled, he lost his enthusiasm for the job of mayor and set about getting himself removed from office. In defiance of the statute requiring the mayor to reside in the city over which he presides, Solari moved twenty-five miles away to Galloway Township, even going so far as to have his official address changed on his driver's license. Once this was discovered, local party officials confronted Solari and found that their ultimatums met with indifference. He had no desire to return, and resigned without finishing his first term in office. At-Large Councilman Phil Guenther stepped up to finish the term as Mayor, and had proved popular enough to be reelected for another term.

(L to R) Brigantine Mayor Phil Guenther, At-Large Council Member Sue
Schilling, Deputy Mayor Ed "Scoop"Kay

Guenther's move up had left open an At-Large seat, which was filled by another
Republican, Sue Schilling. Popular in Brigantine social circles, Schilling and her
husband attended all the right parties and even frequently socialized with John
and Barbara Costello. With the machine behind her, she was able to retain her
seat in the following election, alongside fellow At-Large Councilman Ed "Scoop"
Kay. Kay was an entity unto himself, above much of the political dirt, having rid-
den a jolly disposition and a sincere aw-shucks charm to immense popularity in
Brigantine, and an unassailable position on the council. Scoop and John Costello
were personal friends, socializing frequently and collaborating on political strategy constantly.

So it was that with the top three positions in the city government safely locked up, as well as three of the four ward seats, the Republicans could breathe easy once again and rest in the security of having beaten off the challenge to their dominance. With the elections over and the danger to the party in the past, it was time to relax a bit and enjoy the fruits of victory. It was also time for those who had helped to be repaid. At the front of the line was John Costello, who was approaching his fifties and as tired of the construction industry as he was enamored with the world of city politics.

John had made it no secret that he wanted to take over the Department of Public Works upon the retirement of Robert Gibson Jr., the serving superintendent. Gibson had run the DPW into the ground due to negligence and incompetence, and he was being forced to retire. The general foreman in Costello was just itching to step in and reorganize what was widely seen as an inefficient and disorganized department. Having served as the chief power behind the election of the City Council, which was responsible for the appointment of the new DPW head, Costello had all the political influence he needed to demand the position as his payback. Furthermore, as Municipal Chairman of the Republican Party, the Council was in no position to deny him. In April of 1995, John Costello was appointed Director of Public Works, with the duty of supervising the city's waste collection system, the water facilities, the maintenance of roadways and beaches, any city clean-up operations, and all DPW employees. He would answer to the City Manager, Tom Ciccarone, and would not have the power to hire or fire DPW employees, a right solely reserved by Ciccarone. The DPW essentially consisted of four departments: Public Buildings & Grounds, the Street Dept, the Auto Garage and Recycling. The DPW had been the subject of frequent resident complaints, and with the island in a general state of disrepair and disarray, it was thought that Costello's firm hand and proven organizational skills would help turn things around and get Brigantine headed back on the right track. However, as with most things that are worth accomplishing, it would not be easy.

3

Inmates Running the Asylum

Front entrance of John Costello's offices at the Brigantine Department of Public Works

Even before Costello took over, the problems with the Department of Public Works were many and well known. However, few people were aware of the extent to which things had deteriorated. After all, the stereotype of the lazy, shiftless Public Works employee is one that ranks right up there with the image of the corrupt politician. It has become an archetype at which most people are simply no longer surprised. From the very beginning of his tenure, Costello endeavored to change that stereotype, at least in one small town. However, he certainly had his work cut out for him. When the machinery has been allowed to sit and rust for too long a time, the engine of change can be very tough to get started.

To begin with, the city as a whole was generally dirty and poorly maintained. One of the most common complaints among the residents was the slovenly condition of the streets and public grounds. Overgrown grass and weeds choked the dried out flowerbeds around City Hall, and the children played on weatherbeaten hockey courts littered with broken glass. Trash-strewn streets greeted visitors, and the beautiful sand dunes at the beach, the city's main tourist attraction, were littered with debris, including automobile engines and transmissions. The city's lawns and grounds were poorly and infrequently maintained, and a pile of hundreds of car tires had been allowed to accumulate under the bridge to the island.

Readily apparent problems like these will eventually cause property values to drop, and generally make for an atmosphere of discontent among the taxpayers, but they were nothing compared to the situation Costello discovered in the water department. Immediately after he was hired, John became aware of serious problems involving the city's water facilities that jeopardized the health and welfare of the citizenry. The previous Superintendent of Public Works, Robert Gibson, had been forced to retire and as a consolation prize, his company, Welmet, Inc., was awarded the city's valuable water contracts. Gibson was paid a monthly consulting fee of $1,200 to monitor the testing of the island's drinking water, file the required paperwork with the appropriate government agencies, and to develop maps of the city's infrastructure, such as fire hydrants, manholes, traffic signs and other DPW responsibilities. The problem was that Gibson was not performing any of his contracted tasks. He failed to perform even the most cursory maintenance and left all the government paperwork undone. Not only were there no maps of the island's infrastructure, there were also no records kept of sewer and water maintenance, nor did there exist anyone knowledgeable on the subject within the department. What testing was done was performed by a DPW employee in secret and brought to the ailing Gibson's home for his signature, for which he received a fat check every month. By the time John took over, the island's water facilities had been neglected to the point of abuse. He was so horrified by the water situation in Brigantine that he immediately reported Gibson's breach of his consulting contract to his superior, City Manager Tom Ciccarone. Costello recommended that the city hire a well-known contractor who specialized in managing water systems and had state of the art equipment and information to handle the distribution and testing of water. As a result, Gibson's contract was not renewed, and the city signed a contract with the firm Costello suggested.

John himself eventually created the infrastructure maps, which Gibson had been paid to supply.

One of the most disturbing problems discovered with the water supply was that trash was actually being stored in the city's well houses, which house the pump rooms, from which potable water is pumped for consumption by the residents of the city. Upon making this disturbing discovery, Costello questioned the supervisor of the Water & Sewer Department and was informed that the refuse had been stored in the city water houses by a DPW employee; none other than Bobby Gibson Jr., the son of the very man contracted to keep that water supply safe. The younger Gibson had a reputation for quirkiness, so it came as no surprise to anyone except Costello that Gibson had been patrolling the streets ahead of the trash collectors and picking up any items in which he saw potential resale value. The trash would be stored in the well houses until such time as Gibson found it to be convenient to have a yard sale, at which he would offer up the trash for sale.

One of the potable water pumping houses in which scavenged trash was stored by a DPW employee until he could prepare it for sale.

Costello put a stop to this amazingly unsanitary practice, as well as offering it as another example in persuading the city to choose a new contractor for their water system needs. However, this focus of attention on the water department only uncovered more problems. Because of his background in the electrical industry, John was able to evaluate the motors and pumps at the Water & Sewer Department's facilities. He found that they had been very poorly maintained, which could be very costly to the city, considering that the motors would cost between ten and fifteen thousand dollars each to replace. Further investigation revealed that there were no maintenance schedules implemented for any of the equipment or property in the city. The city's wells and drinking water distribution system were also poorly maintained, and had not been upgraded in approximately twenty years.

Another big problem arose after a regularly scheduled citywide water meter reading was conducted. Upon inspection of the records of these readings, John discovered that many of the billings read zero, others appeared to never have been read, and still others gave the same reading year after year. Under questioning, sheepish employees admitted that it had been the practice under Gibson Sr. to insert five-inch lengths of pipe, called "jumpers", in place of meters that required repairs, until the meter could be brought back to DPW to be fixed. These broken meters were promptly forgotten, resulting in years of free water for "a couple hundred" residential and commercial properties. An entire condominium development was forced to repay back water bills for the flow of water through a four-inch diameter pipe that had been without a meter for more than a year. This situation was discovered when Costello noticed that records reflected no meter for the condominiums, but remembered seeing lights on at night in some windows of the units. Even the local Dairy Queen had her royal name dragged through the mud. A resident telephoned the DPW office to report that she had witnessed the owner of the Dairy Queen, a local plumbing contractor, removing the water meter from the building. Upon inspection, John found that the resident was correct, and notified the police. Nobody can be sure how many of these lucky property holders noticed that they no longer received a water bill, but who can blame them for not complaining? Unfortunately, for them, the free water faucet was turned off under Costello's investigation and continued supervision. However, another problem with the island's water supply arose with an inspection of the city's water towers, which are used to store potable water. One of the island's distinctive sky-blue towers had just been repainted, and in order to hang scaffolding off the side of the tower, holes had been bored in the top of the structure. These holes were never filled, and provided access into the water towers for multitudes of nesting birds. Disgustingly enough, the droppings of all these birds were allowed to contaminate the island's water supply.

Worst of all the water-related problems was the revelation that one part of the island had, and to this day still has, lead pipe connections in the water conduits. Lead is a highly toxic substance, exposure to which can produce a wide range of adverse health effects. Both adults and children can suffer from the effects of lead poisoning, but childhood lead poisoning is much more frequent. Young children under the age of six are especially vulnerable to lead's harmful health effects, because their brains and central nervous system are still being formed. For them, even very low levels of exposure can result in reduced IQ, learning disabilities, attention deficit disorders, behavioral problems, stunted growth, impaired hearing, and kidney damage. At high levels of exposure, a child may become mentally retarded, fall into a coma, and even die from lead poisoning. In adults, lead can increase blood pressure and cause fertility problems, nerve disorders, muscle and joint pain, irritability, and memory or concentration problems. As of this writing, the lead pipe connections still existing in Brigantine have not been addressed.

One of Brigantine's three water storage towers. Non-existent maintenance policies resulted in holes in which birds nested, exposing the island's drinking water to contamination.

Coming into the job as Director, Costello had known that his task would not be an easy one. As he settled into his position, he became aware of just how deep the problems went, and just how out of control the department was. It became apparent that before he could set himself to the task of cleaning up the island, John would first have some major housekeeping to do.

And quite literally, too. The DPW facility was filthy and disorganized. The lawns were poorly maintained, the fencing was broken, the inside of the building was dirty, the fire alarm system was inoperable and the bathrooms were deplorable. On Costello's first day in his new office, one of his first tasks was to remove the quarter inch of filth from the surface of his predecessor's desk. The personnel files of the DPW employees were maintained haphazardly and left unsecured, with workers free to finger through their, or someone else's, file at will. As a result, several employee files were missing. The administrative area of the DPW facility sat at the center of the building, flanked on one side by the Street Department and Public Buildings and Grounds shops, and on the other by the Water & Sewer Department and the auto repair garage. Workers routinely traveled through the administrative center en route to other shops, or to illicitly use the office phones, and left the office area filthy.

The city's vehicles and heavy equipment were in poor condition as well. Costello found that every single truck had body damage, and no records had been kept of any maintenance or repairs to any of the city's rolling stock. The heavy equipment broke down frequently, and there was a recurring problem with damage to DPW's vehicles, such as unexplained dents in doors and bumpers, often occurring soon after an employee had been reprimanded. Questions about damage to the vehicles were seen as harassment by the suspected employee, and were usually followed by a union grievance.

Costello found that there was also a problem with accountability of the city's assets, due to a lack of security. There was no inventory of existing DPW equipment, nor was there any identification marks on any of DPW's tools. Theft was rampant and it seemed like nobody cared. Outside contractors were sometimes called in for special tasks, and they routinely helped themselves to whatever material, tools and equipment they could carry out of the DPW shop. The DPW facility itself was completely unsecured, and people, including city employees, were routinely caught dumping illegally. One brazen, but unlucky, soul was discovered dumping hazardous medical waste by the police. The battle to secure the city yard from regular citizens was hard enough, but the city employees were used to their privileges and perks, and were not going to give them up so easily. One of the biggest theft problems was the municipal gas pump. There was no monitoring system in place to keep track of the gasoline consumption, and the employees were able to freely gas up any vehicle they pleased, with no control exerted over who took how much and for what purpose.

Not all the problems were purposefully malicious. Some were just plain dumb. Just a few months after he started as Director, Costello noticed a large dumpster in the DPW yard, which periodically filled up with scrap metal collected from around the city. To a scrap yard, a dumpster full of metal is worth a pretty penny. Out of curiosity, Costello made inquiries as to the disposition of the contents once a dumpster was filled, and found not corruption but ineptitude. He was informed that the city had a long-term relationship whereby it gave its scrap metal away, for free, to Joe's Auto Wreckage, a company owned by Atlantic County Freeholder Joseph Silipena. Shocked by the inappropriateness of this situation, Costello immediately contacted the mayor and council and alerted them to the tremendous loss being incurred by the city. Silipena was contacted and arrangements were made for payment.

Another problem that probably owed more to laziness than anything else was the situation with the city's drainage system. The city of Brigantine has a catch basin, a whole network of drains throughout the island, which drain the water that would collect during flooding and rain storms. This system requires regular maintenance because it will occasionally fill with sand, preventing the water from draining properly, resulting in frequent flood conditions. Costello discovered that performing this maintenance was seen within DPW as an unpleasant task, so it had gone largely undone. It is impossible to calculate now how much flood damage done to homes and vehicles over the years might have been prevented if only the DPW employees had not perceived this legitimate duty as beneath them. It continued to be difficult for Costello to get employees to perform that task because it required the worker to get into knee or ankle-deep water, which was seen by them as an undesirable job.

From his experience in the construction industry, Costello knew the importance of properly implemented drug and alcohol policies, and was amazed when he learned that the DPW had none in place. The city was paying through the nose for its liability insurance, and remained wide open for a lawsuit in the event an employee caused an accident and proved to be under the influence, which was hardly unthinkable. Once drug and alcohol programs were instituted, the city's insurance rate was lowered significantly, and random drug testing meant doom for those employees who were putting the DPW at risk by showing up for work loaded. One employee failed a drug test and was forced to enter a rehabilitation program that involved restricted duty on the job and after-work counseling sessions. John had personally advised the employee that upon completion of the rehabilitation program, he would be tested once again for drugs. When the results came back from the testing laboratory, Costello says he left the envelope sit on his desk unopened for two days because, *"In my mind it was a no-brainer. He'd been told ahead of time that he'd be tested. Who'd have thought he could possibly fail?"* Fail he did, though. When John opened the envelope and saw that the employee had tested positive for cocaine, he had no more options. He notified City Manager Tom Ciccarone of the situation and the employee was terminated. The alcohol problem in DPW continued to be an ongoing concern, even with the program in place. Bottles of beer and whiskey would be discovered from time to time stashed in different areas of the building.

Around the same time, Costello realized that there was also no sexual harassment policy in place, at a building containing dozens of men and exactly one woman. John's receptionist, Kelly Wilson, worked in the reception area by herself, somewhat isolated from the rest of the building and exposed to the comings and goings of any number of anonymous individuals. Costello was concerned for her safety, and installed a video camera so that the reception area was always monitored in the back office. Kelly initially expressed concern that the camera would be focused on her and monitoring her activities, but John assured her that the camera was focused on the reception area, and that her personal workspace was not even visible. In another attempt to address any danger from within, John arranged for his supervisory staff to attend a course on harassment prevention at the local college. Additionally, the DPW employees were counseled in sexual harassment policy and instructed to remove any potentially offensive materials from the walls and public areas. These policies were a constant battle for Costello to enforce, since it was only his policy and not an official city mandate. Throughout his employment, there was no written personnel policy manual or written policy governing sexual or other unlawful harassment in the workplace.

Another insurance minefield to be traversed was an issue that struck closer to home with John. For years, the DPW had hired the teenage children of Brigantine's influential families as summer helpers. The summer helper program provided many of these teens with their first paying job, in exchange for providing the city with cheap labor for such menial tasks as cutting grass, painting city fences, and emptying the trashcans along the beach. Costello's oldest son had worked as a summer for three seasons, so when John saw the work conditions these kids were exposed to, it really hit home. He found that the teens were frequently left unsupervised, and were permitted to work without proper safety equipment. Furthermore, these fifteen year-olds were frequently assigned tasks involving dangerous machinery, which required a trained operator of no less than eighteen years of age.

Costello, concerned for both the safety of the summer helpers and the city's exposure to costly litigation, completely revamped the summer help program. To his way of thinking, what the kids needed was some real life work experience. Basic skills such as how to show up on time, how to complete tasks as instructed, and how to work safely were not only important at their present job, but would carry over as skills needed for the rest of their lives. Costello organized the teens into what became known as the "Clean Team", using them to scour the island and remove all trash and debris.

He personally supervised their progress and bought the children lunch to encourage and motivate them in their work. The kids learned good work habits and how to take pride in a job well done, as their efforts were noticed and praised by the entire community. John also received a lot of positive feedback from the parents of the children, thanking him for turning the summer job into a positive learning experience.

But by all accounts, the biggest problem in the DPW was the employees. Years of apathy and nepotism had created an environment where the lunatics were running the asylum, resulting in rampant abuse of city resources and funds, not to mention a general state of disrepair around Brigantine. Council members frequently found themselves cornered at social gatherings by irate residents complaining about the conduct and work habits of the city workers. The cliché of driving past roadwork to see a group of public works employees leaning on their shovels and smoking was more than just a cliché in Brigantine, it was a common reality. Even more common was the sight of three or four DPW employees crammed into the cab of a city vehicle, which just cruised around the island all day. Deputy Mayor Kay stated that, *"The supervision there was lacking, very lack-*

ing. We had complaints from citizens, from constituents, about the lack of work being done. Three guys to hold a shovel, three guys in a pickup truck riding around the island. That kind of thing. Just a total lack of supervision."

As bleak as the situation in DPW appeared from the outside, it was even worse from within. Costello found that the department was basically unsupervised, and none of the employees was actually held accountable for their time. They literally just showed up to work, then came and went as they pleased. Employees commonly punched each other's time cards in and out, so there was no way to determine the veracity of the work records. Furthermore, workers were never required to punch out at lunch, so there was no ability to monitor when they went to lunch or how long they took.

Once they were punched in, however, the problems were not over. Under the previous regime, some employees had become accustomed to a certain degree of special treatment. After all, many of them had worked for their daddies for years, and they were used to getting the most desirable assignments and receiving most of the overtime. A certain degree of nepotism is to be expected in any workplace, but in just this generation, there have been no less than thirteen positions held by fathers, sons and brothers of the supervisors. Not exactly a breeding ground for efficiency and good work habits. Workers had grown attached to specified tasks, such as running heavy machinery, and expected to be paid to do nothing when those tasks were not scheduled. If required to perform what they felt to be a less desirable task than that to which they were accustomed, employees would complain and pout, sometimes even filing grievances with the union for harassment.

Some employees had even stronger, and more costly, methods of retaliation. Since the city provided workers with paid sick days, the easiest way to get out of an undesirable assignment was to simply take a few days off. This would serve the double purpose of avoiding the unwanted task, as well as discouraging the boss from assigning similar tasks in the future. If the supervisor persisted in his harassment, the next step was to suffer a "soft tissue injury" on the job and file a Workers' Compensation claim. Again, the city was footing the bill for the employee's entire net pay, so why not? According to DPW records, there was an average of 23 Worker's Compensation claims per year within the department, mostly by the same employees, for alleged soft-tissue problems.

Despite the seemingly constant array of injuries, the DPW employees were quite cavalier regarding the safety practices mandated by law. Many refused to wear the proper safety gear, such as reflective vests for working in traffic. Workers were required to wear these bright orange vests while performing any tasks that involved close proximity to moving vehicles. However, some workers felt the vests were a "*pain in the butt*" and looked "*ridiculous*", so they frequently "forgot" to wear them. This exposed the city to costly litigation by violating the agreement with the insurance carrier, but the fashion sense of the DPW employees was too strong to override easily.

Other employees had to be forced to obey even those safety regulations that would seem to be obviously for their own good. DPW employee Ken Miller was observed cutting wooden pilings with a chainsaw, but wearing no eye protection. When counseled regarding this safety violation, Miller's response was to claim harassment and make the profoundly ridiculous statement, "*I'm blind in one eye already. I'm not crazy enough to lose the other one.*" Such a tale could almost be humorous, if only it were not so sadly indicative of the mindset throughout the department. Not long after this incident, another employee severely injured himself while using a chainsaw.

Especially appalling was the fact that many DPW workers utilized city resources to further their privately owned side businesses. Employees frequently made and received calls in regards to their businesses on the city phones, at city expense. One supervisor directed a subordinate to spend a half a day making telephone calls to Texas, on a DPW phone, in search of wax for the supervisor's candle making business. Another, the trash-collecting son of the former boss, Robert Gibson, operated a private insulation business, and used the DPW facility for storage of his materials. Mike Hopkins, another son of a former supervisor who worked as a city mechanic and served as union shop steward, had a profitable auto repair business operating out of the city garage. Another supervisor stored equipment and materials pertaining to his surfboard making business.

A city employee parks his private business vehicle on the lawn of the
DPW facility while at work.

However, the most outrageous example of this practice had to be the situation
involving the aforementioned employee named Ken Miller. On the job, Miller
generally repaired and maintained the city's irrigation and sprinkler systems, but
he also operated his own private sprinkler system installation business on the side.
It might seem ridiculous to assign an employee work that would create such an
obvious conflict of interest, particularly since he had access to very expensive
sprinkler supplies owned by the city on a day-to-day basis. Perhaps it makes more
sense when we consider the fact that Miller's direct supervisor, Ernie Purdy, had
been a partner with Miller in the sprinkler business.

Besides the obvious impropriety of such situations, additional difficulties arose
out of the fact that the employees with side businesses would drop everything and
leave work precisely at the end of their shift. Unfortunately, a big part of being a
city worker is the fact that people are frequently needed after hours to address
problems that arise around the city during off-hours. Overtime is sometimes
required of the DPW workers in times of emergencies, such as a water main
break, sewer problem, or one of the frequent severe storms suffered on the barrier
island. Overtime was also necessary when public events were conducted in the

city. The side jobs impaired the ability of the DPW employees to fulfill their duties in times of need.

Not every DPW worker was a problem by any stretch of the imagination. But even those who came to work with no agenda other than to do a day's work were subjected to abuse, intimidation and harassment by some of the more maladjusted employees in the department. As a result, morale was so low as to be practically nonexistent. For the past thirty years, the former Director, Robert Gibson Sr., had run things in a very hands-off manner, allowing the senior employees to set policies within their departments. Some employees were allowed to pick their own assignments according to seniority, which resulted in some people always doing the dirty work, and some people always having it easy. This inequity was exploited constantly by the chosen few, leading to dissension in the ranks and a general lack of enthusiasm among even the good employees.

So stepping into the job of Director of the DPW was, in this case, a more daunting task than would usually be the case for a political appointee. However, Costello felt unusually suited to the job, having a history of running a tight ship in the electrical union, where the employees played games that made the city workers look like amateurs. John had been called in before to save a big construction project, such as a casino, that was starting to sink due to inept leadership, and he had achieved success through hard work and determination. He rolled up his sleeves and charged into the DPW job with the same determination, plus an enthusiasm borne of a sincere concern for the welfare his community.

4

Taking the Reins

Much to the displeasure of those who stood to derive continued benefit from the status quo, Costello set about reorganizing the DPW immediately upon taking over. One of his first actions was to negotiate with the Teamsters to extend the working day from seven hours to eight, with a goal of achieving maximum efficiency.

Next, and much more difficult, John began to evaluate each department and the tasks required thereof. He found that the thirty-six or so DPW employees could be divided into three basic groups. The first group would be the good employees, which would be the largest group. The second group consisted of a few people who, if they never came to work again, it would make no appreciable difference. The third group was made up of a small group of employees who caused more problems than they were worth, and by rights, should not even have the job, as they were involved with drug and alcohol abuse, theft, or other improper activities. John made an effort to streamline the DPW staff, cutting loose some deadwood and transferring some personnel to positions where they might be better utilized. The fact that he was able to lower the DPW staff from a bloated thirty-six employees down to twenty-five by 1998, and still show a significant a gain in productivity, seems to bear out Costello's opinions. For the first time, the DPW staff was analyzed according to merit, instead of political influence. For example, one of the first employees to be laid off was the son of Brigantine's Chief of Police.

Once he had reorganized, John began to realize that, with no accountability, there was a certain element in the department that did virtually nothing all day. While the majority of the DPW employees always gave an honest effort, a privileged minority saw it as their inalienable right to goof off all day, and made no attempt to hide their arrogance from their coworkers. Such inequity cannot help but negatively affect worker morale, especially when it receives tacit approval from above. After he implemented policies and procedures that applied to all employees, John observed that morale began to rise. Having changed the operation of the DPW by exposing all the employees to the same treatment, Costello found that a vast majority of the DPW employees looked favorably upon the changes and enjoyed coming to work and having an organized, productive day. Some workers came forward and told John privately that they were glad to see the previously privileged employees finally forced to share the same duties and responsibilities as the rest of their coworkers, and praised the new equity in the department.

One example of such a situation was the case of Nick Manera, who had served under Robert Gibson Sr. for years, and was promoted to Assistant Superintendent of Public Works under Costello. Although a conscientious and dependable employee, Nick had formed the bulk of his experience under the old regime, and John felt his new programs would stand a better chance of success if implemented through a new supervisor with no investment in the previous way of doing things. He had sent numerous memoranda to Ciccarone concerning problems he had observed with Nick Manera's job performance, and favored replacing Manera over continually correcting him. However, John also had no desire to punish or affront Manera, who had served the city well, a fact that deserved consideration in such a delicate situation. It so happened that at the time, the city was in the process of creating a full time recreation/community education program, a new department that would need a leader. That leader was Jim Mogan. Conveniently, Mogan needed an assistant. In a compromise that allowed Costello to replace Manera without causing any undue stress to the former supervisor, John arranged for Nick to be named assistant to the Director of the newly created Recreation Department. As such, Manera would serve as liaison between the DPW and all local city-sanctioned recreation concerns, such as sports teams and civic groups.

Replacing Manera as Costello's right hand man was Ernie Purdy, a longtime foreman in the Streets Dept. who stood far above the pack in terms of responsibility and competence. Purdy had been employed by the DPW since 1981, and served as a supervisor in the Public Buildings & Grounds division since 1986. Having also served in the role of union shop steward, Purdy had gained the respect of the men; an attribute that Costello felt was required of a supervisor. Since John's job requirements placed him in a position of overseeing the entire DPW, he felt it essential that he have a man he could trust with the details of directly supervising the workforce, and Ernie Purdy seemed like the perfect man for the job.

With his staff finalized, John was able to move his attention to the issues within the department that needed to be addressed. One of his first orders of business was to attempt to put a stop to the practice of furthering private businesses on city time, removing the telephones from the DPW shops and banning personal phone calls. He ordered all employees to remove any of their business materials from the DPW facility, and met with Ken Miller to discuss the appearance of a conflict of interest with his irrigation business. John decided to move Miller to a different assignment to avoid any concerns, to which Miller did not react well at all. He bitterly complained that the irrigation systems were "his job" and that Costello had simply "*handed it to someone else.*" Miller suffered no job detriment in terms of reduced salary or benefits as a result of this action, but still saw fit to file a grievance against Costello for harassment. It was found that John was acting fully within the scope of his position in reassigning Miller, and the grievance was acknowledged by the Teamsters Union to be without merit. Costello also repeatedly demanded that mechanic Mike Hopkins immediately cease repairing non-city vehicles in the DPW garage, but was met with constant resistance, and noted that the practice continued throughout his entire tenure as Director.

In an attempt to curb the sick leave abuses, John had a special phone line installed and required the employees to call the DPW in the morning if they were not going to come to work. This allowed supervisors time so that plans could be shifted and a minimal amount of time wasted waiting around for a crewmember that was not going to show up. He advised Ciccarone and members of city council that certain DPW employees were taking days off when they were not sick, as a form of protest, and that some employees had submitted bogus claims for Workers' Compensation benefits by alleging exaggerated or non-existent injuries. The ongoing problems with sick leave and Workers' Comp. abuse was discussed with the Teamsters officials, and it was agreed that Costello was permitted under the union's collective bargaining agreement to verify and check any sick leave or Worker's Comp. claims asserted by employees. Once he began to enforce the agreement, workers found it much more difficult to abuse the system. The sick leave abuses never really stopped, since the city manager wouldn't institute a policy to bring it under control, but by requiring doctor's notes and being vigilant about following up on all claims, Costello was able to curtail the problem with Worker's Compensation. During his tenure as director, John was able to reduce the number of Worker's Comp. claims from twenty-five during his first year on the job, down to seven in his last year.

After restructuring the departments and redistributing the work force, John made sure the supervisors were accountable for the whereabouts and productivity of their men. No longer did the men get to select their assignments according to seniority. Costello implemented a computerized work order system, which prioritized and assigned the tasks according to the size of the job and the resources and manpower required. The work order system also created accountability, allowing Costello to keep track of the job assignments, the length of time the task was expected to take, and the cost of the project to the city. When timetables were not met, or budgets exceeded, John could use the work orders to look into any delays and determine if the projected time frame was unrealistic, or if there was a problem with the employee's productivity. When a task projected for completion in four or five hours took several days, Costello would investigate. Many times, these investigations yielded little but accusations of harassment. Some of the men were not used to such close supervision, and reacted defensively when questioned. John found that the legitimate workers quickly became accustomed to the new system and began to flourish in a way that was unthinkable under the previous regime. The men were encouraged to improve themselves and their earning potential by attending school for special licenses and permits, which John felt would raise the standard of the department.

The battle to secure the DPW yard was constant and ongoing. John had gates installed, changed locks, and secured the dumping area. Still problems with theft and misuse of DPW resources continued. It was a never-ending struggle to deter some employees from repeatedly attempting to dump trash at night when the yard was closed. Costello brought to Ciccarone's attention the security issues he had observed with relation to the city's gasoline pumps, and in response to his findings, the city purchased a computerized gasoline dispensing system, requiring a key to gain access to the pumps. However, the situation continued to be a problem, as certain employees made a hobby of habitually "losing" their keys. This required replacements to be issued, and as a result, nobody could be sure exactly how many gasoline keys existed, and in whose hands they lay.

Finally, there was the DPW property itself. The poor condition of the department's buildings and grounds was hardly the tone Costello wished to set for his campaign to clean up the rest of the island. John took action to get the property cleaned up, and put policies and systems into place so that the facility was regularly maintained. Additionally, he took steps to see that the DPW personnel files were properly secured, and instituted new rules requiring that all DPW employees, besides supervisors and those with permission, stay out of the administrative area. Although most found that the clean-up efforts drastically improved the condition and image of the department, some employees resented the changes. They resisted the improvements John was making, and felt it was beneath them to paint a wall or clean the floor on a rainy day. Previously, if the piece of equipment an employee regularly operated was not needed for that day's assignments, that employee just sat around the shop all day and did nothing. Costello developed a system under which the employees whose primary duties were not utilized would perform needed maintenance to the DPW facility. This outraged some workers, who complained bitterly. Some even went so far as to allege harassment, even though such assignments fell squarely within the scope of their job description. As obvious as it would seem to anyone of even average intelligence, John actually had to defend himself by pointing out that cleaning and maintaining a facility that generates so much dirt is an ongoing process, and not a single event.

With his own house in order, so to speak, John could now set himself to the task of cleaning up Brigantine. He set loose his newly created "Clean Team" and had them scour the island until it shined. Gradually, signs of improvement began to appear around the island. The streets were cleaner, and formerly overflowing litter baskets were emptied regularly. Public grounds were properly cut and trimmed. The concrete fountain in the traffic circle at the center of town was refurbished and returned to working order. New paint jobs on all the fire hydrants, lifeguard shacks and pump houses also helped add to Brigantine's new, cleaner image. The island was beginning to sparkle again, and soon the difference was quite noticeable.

Once the DPW had rid Brigantine of its initial layer of filth, it became apparent that the blame for the litter problem rested not only with Public Works, but also with some private residents. It was found that residents were carelessly disposing of their garbage, resulting in torn open bags and wind-blown trash all over the streets. Costello developed an aggressive system under which the offending resident was warned about the situation, and given a certain amount of time to address the problem. If it did not improve promptly, the resident could be cited with a summons for municipal court and fined. In the case of rental properties, the property owner was held responsible for problem tenants. Ticketing the trash violations was an effective tactic in the short run, but proved to carry with it problems of its own. It certainly got everyone's attention very quickly, and definitely had a dramatic effect on the trash problem. It also helped to heighten public awareness of the need to keep the city clean. However, John found it difficult to deal with the constant distraction of residents complaining about being cited and demanding special dispensation. As time went on, enforcing the tickets became more and more of a battle, as John was faced with interference from above, as well.

Empty lots strewn with trash and overgrown weeds were another "quality of life" problem around the island. After warning the property owners and allowing them a reasonable period to correct the problems themselves, John had DPW workers clean, clear and, in some cases, even fill the lots. The cost was then assessed to the property owner. Abandoned and junked vehicles were removed from both public streets and private properties. This was thanks to a long-forgotten ordinance, which Costello brought to the attention of the police, enabling them to remove the vehicles and get rid of many eyesores around town.

Once he felt he had the most immediate problems under control, John began a project to develop a book of all needed repairs for the entire island. Brigantine contained fifty-two miles of streets, which were all paved and in various states of disrepair and deterioration. Over a period of months, John reviewed every single street on the island and developed a grading system with which the streets were prioritized in order of most urgently needed repairs. This book allowed the city to organize its maintenance system and develop a capital budget for complete renovation of the streets in a cost-efficient manner. John knew from his own experience as a resident that some of the streets in town were in pretty bad shape, and made it a priority to get them fixed.

By all accounts, Costello had been a rousing success in his first two years as Director of Public Works. City officials all found the city to be much cleaner and the DPW to be more organized and productive. Now, instead of complaints, Council members were hearing from residents about how pleased they were with the city's turnaround. Third Ward Councilman Sam Storino heard many different concerns from his constituents, and found that once notified, John had the projects immediately completed to the satisfaction of the resident, which went a long way at re-election time. Taxes may rise and fall, but the candidate who can get your streetlight fixed, or have the pothole in front of your house filled is the one you are most likely to remember in the voting booth.

Deputy Mayor Ed "Scoop" Kay said that Costello instituted *"an amazing program to clean up…not just the streets, but every property the City owned."* Everyone to whom Kay spoke said that the city was the cleanest it had ever been, and he shared that opinion. The Deputy Mayor also stated on the record that he felt the DPW kept improving every year under Costello.

Residents of Brigantine showed their appreciation by sending letters to the local papers and to city officials, praising the job the DPW had done in beautifying the island. In one letter to the newspaper, a waterfront resident wrote about how she complained to her Councilman about the debris and rubbish left in her area after a particularly bad storm. She went on to say, *"The next day, John Costello, the Superintendent of Public Works, appeared with his "Clean Team" and extensive cleanup was under way. When the many capable workers, street sweepers, vacuums, etc. were finished, Harborview Villas fairly sparkled!"*

Another resident wrote a letter to the paper entitled, *"I'm Starting to Like Brigantine Again!"* He praised the improvements around town and had more compliments for the "Clean Team", *"I also saw something that is not seen much in our country anymore. Men with brooms, shovels and scrapers working to cut weeds and growth from curbing and other places where machines cannot normally reach or get at. This crew, I later found, is dispatched to different areas that have these problems and is called the 'Brigantine Clean Team'. Heck, with the way they approached and did their work, and with the gusto they did it with, they should be called 'The Mean Clean Machine of Brigantine'. Great work, men, keep at it!"*

That same resident went on to describe a visit to the DPW office, *"I had to express my feelings to the Superintendent of Public Works on the excellent manner he was handling his duties. There again, I was impressed by the look of the Public Works building; newly painted, windows cleaned, sidewalks swept and shrubs trimmed. Upon entering, I again was astounded to see a brightly lit, clean, business-type office. I asked to see Mr. Costello and received prompt attention. He spoke to me at length, answering my questions and also telling me his thoughts. He asked for my opinion on some of his thoughts and ideas, to which he listened attentively. He thanked me for my observations and comments and suggested that I stop in again if the need arose at any time. All this, I must add, was time he gave freely, since when I left his office it was well past five o'clock. To Mr. Costello…thank you, and keep up the splendid work.*

Sentiments like these typified the cards and letters that residents wrote in praise of the job he was doing, and John kept them all in what he called his "Atta Boy" file. He also received numerous letters from private and public organizations, and even from city employees, commending his performance. He took great pride in having had a hand in turning things around for Brigantine, and felt even better for having his efforts noticed.

Soon, word got around about the big changes happening in Brigantine, and even some of the local media took notice. Don Williams, host of a local issues-driven AM talk radio show on area station WOND, commented several times on the improvements he'd seen on the island, as well as broadcasting calls from Brigantine residents expressing how thrilled they were with the city's new look.

In the summer of 1997, at the request of Mayor Guenther and Deputy Mayor Kay, Costello escorted Jay Lamont, host of a Philadelphia-based real estate talk show, on a tour of the island. On the following Sunday's broadcast, Lamont described Brigantine as *"the cleanest city I have ever seen."* and, *"not just clean, but immaculate."*

About one year into his tenure as Director, Costello asked his direct supervisor, City Manager Tom Ciccarone, for an evaluation of his performance. Ciccarone told John in no uncertain terms, *"I love you, you've turned the Department around!"*

Ciccarone did not restrict his praise for Costello to merely private expressions of affection, however. In his 1998 budget presentation to City Council, the City Manager reported, *"John Costello, the Director of the Department of Public Works, has made the DPW more efficient and accountable than it has ever been. In 1997 Public Works established a new computerized work order system and completed over three thousand work orders for the year, with less full-time staff than the department had 25 years ago. Also during 1997, Public Works implemented a centralized and computerized fuel system, completed the removal of all the city's underground storage tanks, built the new tot playground to serve the children of the golf course neighborhood, built two new bocce courts and rebuilt one hockey rink at the 42nd Street recreation complex. Additionally, 1997 saw the Department of Public Works continue to make progress in keeping our city clean and beautiful. I would like to thank John and his support staff—Ernie Purdy, Kelly Wilson and the workers of Teamsters Local 331 for the team effort which is making the Department successful."*

5

Public Jerks

As wonderful a job as most people seemed to agree John was doing, not everyone was so pleased with all the changes. First, there was an element among the DPW workers who responded to Costello and his new programs with resistance and resentment. In any work environment that undergoes a change, there will commonly be a number of employees who are unhappy, or who take a little longer to get used to the new way of things. Such normal feelings existed among a few of the DPW employees, and John worked together with those individuals to try to make the transition easier. Such employees were not the problem. A supervisor who is unable to work together with employees to resolve legitimate differences does not deserve the position. The problem was with a group known colloquially as the Wolfpack.

The Wolfpack was a group of employees who had been very comfortable with the former regime, and had no intention of cooperating with any new plan, especially one that required them to begin carrying their own weight in the department. The group was made up of four employees: **Bobby Gibson**, the trash-picker whose father Costello replaced as Director; **Mike Hopkins**, the union shop steward and son of another former DPW department head; **Ken Miller**, the aforementioned sprinkler entrepreneur, and **Joe Lombardo**, a more recent hire, who had gravitated towards birds of a similar feather.

These four saw in Costello the end of their long-running gravy train and went on the counterattack. Having had it so good for so long, they interpreted the effort to increase efficiency in the DPW as a threat to their jobs, and perhaps rightly so. Under Gibson's father, they had become accustomed to favorable treatment, but were suddenly subjected to the same policies and procedures as the other DPW workers. This was the first time some of them had been exposed to a real work environment and the shock left them frightened and confused. Instead of making an effort to be a part of the new and improved DPW, the Wolfpack turned its collective fear and confusion into rage focused on Costello. To them, John was not simply reorganizing DPW in an attempt to improve the island and save the city money. He was an abusive and overbearing ogre, whose sole purpose in life was to make them miserable and eventually take away their jobs. When any of the four received a memo or were counseled regarding their performance, they became angry and suspicious, accusing Costello of "setting them up" to be fired. Eventually, like a parasite whose grip on its host is threatened, they fought back.

From John's point of view, the Wolfpack seemed to have undertaken an organized conspiracy to undermine and disrupt DPW operations, in an effort to resist and ultimately end Costello's control of the department. Their agenda was to create as much confusion and dissension as possible, as well as taking any opportunity to file a grievance against John with the Teamsters Union. For the most part, the union found their grievances to be without merit, but reality failed to deter the Wolfpack. They were filing papers and establishing a pattern. Their goal was not to oust Costello with a single complaint, but instead to build up a file of grievances against him which, when taken collectively, would create the impression that Costello was abusive toward the men. They referred to this process of constant written complaints as *"killing trees."* One of the Wolfpack's favorite complaints was that Costello harassed them through undesirable work assignments.

John actually had very little direct contact with the workers, with regard to work assignments. Instead, he delegated the assignments to Ernie Purdy, his assistant, who then dealt with the employees directly on a regular basis. Purdy handed out job assignments and relayed criticisms concerning tasks that were not satisfactorily completed. The employees' contact with the Director consisted generally of memos from Costello with regard to performance or conduct. Gibson, Hopkins, Miller and Lombardo each had numerous memos criticizing their work performance and productivity, which they conveniently explained away as harassment by Costello. They viewed any memo as an attempt to create a "paper trail" with which they could be threatened, assuming, much like the thief who fears nothing more than being robbed, that John was undertaking the same strategy as they themselves employed against him. It never occurred to them to consider that any criticism could possibly be legitimate.

Most people with a minimal level of experience in the working world are familiar with the concept of a chain of command. John stuck to the chain of command in DPW, in which he communicated his concerns to the men through Ernie Purdy, their direct supervisor. The Wolfpack, in a combination of lack of real work experience and wishful thinking, chose to interpret this as a sign of fear. They comforted themselves by alleging that John was too cowardly to confront them directly with his concerns. However, whenever Costello personally approached any of them, they would consistently clam up and study the floor. Only later would they file union grievances, or develop mysterious nagging injuries. Any attempt at a resolution through normal conversation was met with downcast eyes and mumbled complaints about production expectations being too high. However, among an audience of co-workers, the Wolfpack grew much more loquacious, openly urging other employees to join their efforts. When persuasion and propaganda failed, they would just as happily resort to harassment in order to win converts.

Having a group of malcontents on the crew can be a tough situation for any supervisor. Having that group undertake an organized vendetta against the supervisor would be described by most as intolerable, as well as somewhat bizarre. However, when that group of conspirators begins to actively recruit among the other workers to join their crusade, the entire work environment has been undermined and jeopardized. At the slightest sign of discontent in any employee, the Wolfpack would swing into action. They would immediately begin soliciting that employee to file a grievance against Costello, in an effort to establish a pattern and build a case for his removal as Director. Employees who hesitated were intimidated and harassed, even to the point of being threatened with physical violence. Other employees who were perceived as friendly or supportive to Costello were singled out, labeled as "rats" and tormented by the Wolfpack. A rat was any employee who refused to go along with their agenda, or who complained about their inappropriate behavior. Ken Miller defined a rat as *"Somebody who runs back and tells the boss what's going on."* Apparently, until Costello took over, the DPW had obviously operated under the philosophy that the boss did not need to know what was going on.

According to Miller, whenever any employee complained about the conduct of the Wolfpack, the information would make it back to them through what he termed, *"the rat grapevine."* From there, they would *"figure out the trail"* and identify the complainer, who would be labeled a rat and ostracized. Once someone had been identified as a rat, that employee would be shunned and intimidated. The harassment varied from threats and name-calling to throwing away an employee's tools, damaging a personal vehicle, and worse. Anyone doubting the seriousness with which the Wolfpack maintained their rat grapevine should consider the fact that even Mike Hopkins' brother, Fred, had been branded with the label. When questioned how Fred Hopkins had earned the rat label, Miller said, *"I don't know that for a fact. When things get back to the boss, they can only go one way. It's easy to figure out the trail."* One can only wonder what types of activities are taking place during work hours that make it of such paramount importance that the boss not find out.

Even the direct supervisor of the men, Ernie Purdy, admitted that some of the employees made derogatory comments or threats toward him because he was perceived as an ally of Costello. Purdy called Costello and told him that Gibson's neighbor had told Purdy's wife that Gibson had said, the first chance he got, he intended to *"cut Ernie's throat."* John advised Purdy to notify the police, but Ernie dismissed it as an idle threat. Other employees were ordered not to speak to Costello, and they would be terrorized if they did not comply with the Wolf-pack's demands. One DPW employee even suffered harassment at his home. Miller and Hopkins had the nerve to pull into the employee's driveway and demand that he remove a political sign from his lawn, since the advertised politician, Senator William Gormley, was perceived by the Wolfpack to be a supporter of Costello. The brave DPW employee refused to bow to the pressure, and as a result, was repeatedly the subject of harassment and threatening behavior by Wolfpack members. Even the teenaged summer helpers were not immune to this treatment. The Wolfpack made sure to spew their venom within the hearing of the impressionable youngsters, and bestowed favorable treatment upon those kids whom, seeking the approval of the older guys, parroted back their anti-Costello rhetoric.

The ringleader of the Wolfpack was definitely Bobby Gibson. Not exactly possessing the aptitude one might imagine in the alpha male of a Wolfpack, Gibson drew his basis for leadership from the fact that his daddy had been the boss, something he never let the other employees forget. Gibson lorded his privilege over the rest of the DPW workers with an arrogance that belied his meager achievements. Ernie Purdy, a longtime DPW supervisor, stated that Gibson would threaten and belittle other employees, attempting to use his father's power against anyone with the temerity to challenge his nonexistent authority. When asked why some employees feared retribution from Gibson's father, Ernie Purdy explained, *"That's a gimme, because if your son is working for me and he's a little son of a bitch, I'm going to have a real hard time telling you, look, your kid's a bum, ok?"* DPW employees say he was allowed to do pretty much as he pleased for years, which explains his hostile response to the changes instituted by Costello.

Tall and gangly, Gibson cuts something of an intense profile and has been described by co-workers as "scary." Most who described him thusly were quick to qualify that statement, however. It was not that Gibson was scary in the sense that he was tough or intimidating, as much as in the sense of being creepy. Less a wolf than a hyena or jackal, Gibson was one of those fellows who make up for certain deficiencies with a particular fondness for weapons, a fact that made him even more potentially dangerous. He was known by most of his co-workers to be a collector of guns and knives, and had a reputation for handling them in an unsafe manner. Costello was informed by DPW workers that Gibson, prior to John's hiring, had even brought a gun into the Public Works facility and had fired it through a wall into the auto repair garage, with no consideration of who might be on the other side of the wall. Other employees recounted tales of Gibson constructing homemade pipe bombs in the DPW shop, which he then took down to the public beach to detonate.

After several employees complained to Costello about Gibson, John felt it was time to sit down and have a talk with this seemingly troubled employee. Gibson exhibited a hostile attitude from the very start and seemed completely unaware of any problems with his behavior. He viewed himself as having been victimized and unfairly harassed by Costello. In the past, whenever Gibson Sr. had tried to control his son's antics at work, Gibson Jr. would complain to his mother, who would then chastise the father, resulting in essentially no discipline for young Bobby, according to one of his former supervisors who was close with the family. Gibson had become accustomed to this arrangement, and had genuine difficulties adjusting to the weight of accountability finally resting upon his shoulders.

Those difficulties manifested themselves in increasingly bizarre behavior, directed at both his supervisors and co-workers. For example, Gibson liked to torment his working partner by having breakfast at his parents' house while his partner waited outside in the city truck. In another bit of senseless cruelty, Gibson would pull the truck in front of his partner's ex-wife's house and blow the horn, pulling away when she came to the door. In another display of maturity, on one of the many occasions when he was displeased with a job assignment, Gibson sat in the break room and filled his mouth with coffee cake, which he then proceeded to spray out of his mouth, all over the area. Upon being instructed to clean his disgusting and childish mess, he refused and complained to his father that he was being picked on by his supervisor.

Other instances of Gibson's inability to play well with others were incidents in which he similarly abused, threatened and harassed other employees. Gibson's supervisor in the Water Department produced handwritten notes regarding Gibson's behavior. *"He was asked to clean his truck one day, and he threw a temper tantrum, ranting, raving and throwing objects. One object was a three foot piece of copper tubing that almost hit Gary and myself."*

Behavior such as this made Gibson extremely unpopular with his co-workers, and finally came to a head when the entire staff of the Water & Sewer Dept. got together and announced they would no longer work with him. They had generated a six-page list of complaints about young Gibson, complete with descriptions of his behavior signed by his co-workers and an account of the results of a previous attempt to resolve these problems while Gibson's father was in charge. The supervisor of the Water & Sewer Dept, Carmen Danunzio, went to John and demanded that Gibson be transferred out of his department because none of the other employees wanted to work with him. He had previously complained of Gibson, *"He has no respect for anyone in the Public Works building, not even his father. I have brought this problem to his father's attention and it did nothing but create more problems for my men and I. It is my opinion that a 25 year old man who does the things he does should seek mental help."*

In the words of Ernie Pudy, *"The whole department got together. It was like a big coup."* After conducting meetings with the Water & Sewer Dept. employees, John agreed to transfer Gibson into the Street Department, which brought on a completely new set of challenges. First of all, Gibson wouldn't go. He seemed to think that if he simply resisted for long enough, the issue would be dropped. Gibson had been asked to remove his personal belongings from his former locker in the Water Department facility, but had repeatedly refused. Finally, John had the lock cut off the locker and boxed up Gibson's belongings, which ominously included rifle-cleaning equipment, which he then delivered to the Street Dept. facility. However, Ken Miller, another Wolfpack member, later claimed to have inadvertently thrown the box away, although no trace of it could be found in any trash container. Several days later, Gibson filed a grievance with the union, as well as criminal charges with the police, alleging that John had illegally removed his property, and that "valuables" had been taken. Listed among the missing items were of course cash, jewelry, electronics, and in a strange and twisted claim, nude photos of Gibson and his wife. These grievances were investigated and found to be without merit by the City Manager. The criminal complaint was dismissed for lack of a factual basis. Ciccarone made what he considered a fair offer to reimburse Gibson for what he claimed he had lost, but Gibson rejected that offer. Presumably, Gibson placed a high value on those nude photographs. Ciccarone then dismissed the grievance and told the union that he did not think the grievance had been filed for the reason that the process was in place, and instead felt that Gibson was trying to construct a civil claim. The process cost the city over four thousand dollars in legal fees, as well as the lost productivity of the people who had to waste time partaking in Gibson's folly. Ciccarone told the union to stop encouraging members to file frivolous complaints, a practice that was to continue unabated.

In addition to the incident where he threatened to cut Ernie Pudy's throat, Gibson also once drove to Purdy's home in a rental car and sat outside the house at night, just silently staring. Purdy was unaware of the ominous stalker's identity until he wrote down the tag number and had it traced to a car service where Gibson had rented a vehicle. Purdy says that while he did not previously take Gibson seriously, the incident was enough to cause him to be concerned for the safety of his wife and children. Shortly thereafter, John sent Ciccarone a memo advising that he felt Gibson may be dangerous and potentially violent. He received no reply and no action was taken.

On another occasion, Costello and Purdy drove into the DPW yard during the workday and discovered that Gibson was back at the yard, instead of out cutting grass, as he had been assigned with the rest of the crew. The department had a set procedure for what time the workers were supposed to come back to the yard to clean up the equipment and put everything away for the next day's work, so John was curious as to why Gibson was back at the yard early. There had been a problem with the crew falling behind on the cutting schedule and John was concerned that possibly there had been a breakdown or possibly some other problem. He and Purdy drove over to Gibson and asked him why he was back at the yard early. Gibson, as was his practice, just shrugged his shoulders, stared at the ground and refused to answer, like a child hoping to wait out an adult's anger.

Costello informed Gibson that he was expected to comply with the rules just like the rest of the crew, and that to stop working early for no good reason was not acceptable. Gibson replied by hissing at Costello, *"I'm sick of your fucking shit."* Hardly the response of a well-adjusted individual. Instead of allowing himself to be baited, Costello retreated to his office to give the situation a chance to cool down and determine the proper response to Gibson's outburst. He finally decided to suspend Gibson for two days without pay for insubordination. In response, Gibson filed a criminal complaint against Costello, alleging that John had approached him in an intimidating manner, and that he felt he was going to be assaulted. There were three witnesses to the incident, and none of them substantiated Gibson's claims, not even fellow Wolfpack member Joe Lombardo.

In an attempt to resolve the complaint, Costello attended court-recommended mediation and expressed a desire to start his work relationship with Gibson over with a clean slate, just shake hands and put the trouble behind them. He tried to explain his reasons for Gibson's suspension and open lines of communication so further incidents would not occur. Unfortunately, Gibson came to the mediation with an agenda and behaved in a hostile and vindictive manner, which led the mediator to conclude that the session was a waste of time. In fact, Gibson went as far as to have a confederate hide at the mediation and videotape Costello's arrival, after which Gibson attempted to use the videotape as evidence that John was using the city vehicle to conduct private business. This sham cost the city over ten thousand dollars in legal fees, plus lost productivity.

In one of his most unbelievable anecdotes, Gibson had been assigned to the task of removing algae growth from a meadow near the beach. Neighbors had complained about a bad odor from algae growing on stagnant pools of water in the area, but the area fell under the category of wetlands, and could not legally be filled in or excavated without special permit. The only remedy was to have a DPW worker go in and physically skim the algae growth off the top of the pool and then vacuum out the water. Possibly not the most pleasant task in the world, but one that was necessary. When Gibson received this assignment, which is perfectly within the scope of his job, he felt he was being harassed, and took steps to ensure he would not be assigned this task again. Costello was only a few blocks away from the area when he heard the distress call going out over the radio. Gibson claimed to be stuck in the ankle-deep mud, and felt so endangered by the situation that he radioed 911 for assistance. Just to be clear, he was not calling for help because of his truck being bogged down in the mud. He was calling 911 because he himself was physically stuck in the ankle-deep mud, despite the fact that he had been provided with hip wader boots. How he was able to place the call while struggling in the mud like a dinosaur stuck in a tar pit is unknown, but Brigantine's four-wheel-drive beach permit inspector was the first to respond to what she assumed to be a sincere request for assistance. She found herself dumbfounded by the stunning lack of shame exhibited by the DPW employee as he piteously wailed for help in inch-deep water. Moments later, Costello himself arrived on the scene, expecting to find a legitimate emergency. Instead, he found Gibson sitting safely on the side of the meadow, with his usual sheepish grin in place. Police and fire vehicles and personnel were dispatched to assist Gibson, another wasted expenditure of taxpayers' money. Fortunately, no resident legitimately required emergency assistance at the time. Gibson then called the Occupational Safety and Health Administration (OSHA) and reported that he had been put in a dangerous situation in which he could have been injured. OSHA made a surprise visit to the DPW facility and met with Costello, Purdy, Gibson and union steward Hopkins. The actual area in question was then inspected by OSHA, and it was determined that there was no safety issue.

Problems like these arose only when Gibson deigned to show up for work. Luckily for his co-workers and supervisors, but not so luckily for the taxpayers, Gibson was also one of the leaders in DPW at filing Worker's Compensation claims and abusing sick leave. When Gibson's pattern of abuses began to become apparent to John, he went to the City Manager to bring the problem to his attention. John found that Ciccarone was well aware of the situation, and furthermore, that it had existed long before Costello took over the reigns at DPW. It almost became a joke, with the City Manager and the Director of Public Works playing a game of "Can You Top This?" in competition to see who had the worst Bobby Gibson story. Ciccarone reached back to 1991 to tell John the story of Gibson going out on Worker's Comp. for a back injury, only to have it discovered that he was actually using the time to build a home in nearby Leeds Point. He followed it up with the even more impressive tale of Gibson taking off another six months or so, with pay of course, due to yet another back injury. When that claim ran out, Gibson immediately followed it up with another extended paid leave, citing psychological disability. While no one disputed the legitimacy of Gibson's mental problems, to place the burden of paying for such an obviously pre-existing condition upon the backs of the taxpayers is completely unfair.

On April 1, 1997, Costello issued a memorandum addressed to the Public Works field personnel, which listed the number of sick and personal days taken by each employee in the first quarter of that year. Number one with a bullet was Bobby Gibson, with an astounding sixty-three missed, but fully paid, workdays. This number becomes even more shocking when considering that the entire first quarter of the year consists of only ninety days, approximately twenty of which are weekends or holidays. By comparison, the next highest total number of missed days, a still unacceptable thirty-six, might seem almost tame, if it were not for the fact that the totals dropped sharply after that from thirty-six down to six.

Having gone unchallenged in his poor work habits for so long, one can almost understand Gibson's outrage when Costello took over and began to hold him responsible for his behavior. The first clash of wills came when Gibson called out sick the day before he was scheduled to go on vacation, but showed up that afternoon to pick up his paycheck. By this time, John had grown weary of Gibson's constant absenteeism, and since Gibson exhibited no signs of actually being ill when he arrogantly showed up to retrieve his pay, the city refused to pay him for the day off. Gibson responded by filing a grievance that was dismissed when Costello showed that he had the right to question the legitimacy of an employee's claim of illness if evidence showed otherwise.

Another of Gibson's bizarre habits was to call out sick, but then show up at a work site to distract and bother the other DPW employees while they worked. One former DPW employee speculated that it brought Lakes a perverse joy to watch the other men work for their pay while he himself was paid for the day off. This becomes even more unusual when one is reminded that Gibson did not reside in Brigantine, but instead in Leeds Point, a significant distance away, even by car.

In 1998, the situation came to a head when Costello reached the limits of his patience and began to take proactive measures to curb the rampant sick leave abuse. Gibson had once again called out sick under questionable circumstances. After receiving permission from Ciccarone, John and Ernie Purdy hopped into a city truck and took a drive out to Leeds Point. As they approached Gibson's home, they saw an obviously healthy Gibson outside with some friends, building a front porch onto his house. Gibson saw the city truck and immediately became enraged, screaming obscenities and approaching the vehicle menacingly. Exercising discretion, Costello drove away before anything untoward could occur. He reported the incident to Ciccarone and recommended that Gibson not be paid for the day.

The next day Gibson began a one-man media blitz attack on Costello. He called the Don Williams radio show and, while posing as a caller named "Luke", proceeded to level allegations of mismanagement at the Brigantine DPW. "Luke" claimed to have plenty of inside information, and informed the listening audience that any positive changes that happened in Brigantine were a sole result of the efforts of the DPW workers, and furthermore that Costello was on vacation every time there was a problem. "Luke" could not tell Williams how he came by his information, but to bolster his credibility, Gibson later called back, this time using his own name, to confirm all of the claims made by the courageous "Luke". Gibson also claimed that Costello had harassed him by driving past his house, and made various other derogatory public comments regarding his supervisor.

Williams was forced to cut Gibson off when he began a Unabomber-esque diatribe, rambling about dictators and secret government conspiracies. *"Another point I want to get across to all the politicians, that they've known I've been talking to some of these people that I wanted to give up where they won. They won. I don't care anymore. That's what I think they're worried about is because I don't care anymore. But I do want people to know that they are getting in a bad situation by electing these people. They say jeopardy. I mean, their Councilmen, what I wanted to get across, the Councilmen are jeopardizing their own credibility by backing up this man and doing that. They say Twilight Zone? The Council sits there and says yes, yes, yes to whatever dictatorship that is, I don't know what's in charge, Ciccarone, or Costello, because he's, you know, the campaign manager. I don't know who has more power, who really gives the okay for everything, but all it is is a yes Council. These men…"* At that point, Williams had reached the limit of his patience and ended the call. However, Gibson had not yet concluded his broadcast day. Apparently still recognizing his lack of credibility, Bobby then had his sister, Becky Gibson, call the radio show. Under the alias "Donna", she made comments regarding what a terrible person in general John Costello was, also alleging that the men at DPW were all bums and alcoholics who forced poor Bobby Gibson to do all the work. Having discovered an easily accessible but safely anonymous forum from which he could attack Costello with no danger of consequences, Gibson took to calling the Don Williams show regularly with his complaints, and had calls aired several times. The fact was used to arrogantly taunt Costello, such as when some anonymous scribe had written "Luke and Donna, Perfect Together" on the chalkboard hanging in the Street Dept garage.

Gibson also had his sister approach the City Manager and make a complaint that Costello had deliberately attempted to cause a traffic accident with her. Becky Gibson angrily claimed that she had been driving behind a city vehicle driven by Costello, also identifying Ernie Purdy as the passenger, when Costello had knowingly jammed on his brakes, seeking to cause her to crash into his rear. John, of course, had no knowledge of the situation until informed of the claims by Ciccarone. Neither Costello nor Purdy could recall even seeing Gibson's sister in traffic, let alone attempting vehicular homicide against her.

A day or two after the traffic incident, John signed a complaint against Gibson for spitting on his wife's car. At the time, Barbara Costello was employed at city hall as City Clerk, and on the day in question, the DPW workers were cutting the lawn at city hall. Unaware of Gibson's growing animosity toward her husband, when Barbara witnessed a DPW employee walk by her car and spit on it, she was shocked and called John to complain. Instead of confronting Gibson and possibly being provoked into an ugly incident, Costello signed a criminal complaint against Gibson. The parties went to court and were sent to mediation once again, where it was determined that one is legally entitled to spit upon another person's belongings. There is no real enforceable law against such a disgusting and disrespectful act.

Soon thereafter, John was told by Ciccarone that the city's labor attorney had informed him that Gibson was out on psychiatric leave. Since it was suspected that Gibson might be dangerous to those he saw as his enemies, John was advised to be on guard and try to avoid any confrontations. As he made it a habit to avoid Gibson in any case, this was not much of a problem.

However, there was still the rest of the Wolfpack to deal with. Contending with Gibson for the title of "Biggest Troublemaker" was Mike Hopkins, another disgruntled son of a former DPW supervisor. Employed right out of high school in 1977, under the job title of Labor/Operator/Driver, he later trained as an auto mechanic, and was transferred to fleet maintenance in 1983. Hopkins also served as the union shop steward for the DPW during Costello's tenure. The basic function of the shop steward is to serve as liaison between the Teamsters Union and DPW management, hearing grievances from employees and resolving on-the-job disputes. It is an extra duty, but not one that alleviates normal work responsibilities. Hopkins communicated with and answered to the union concerning union business, but otherwise remained a normal DPW employee under the direct supervision of Costello.

Of course, Hopkins saw things differently. He seemed to view his position as shop steward as an opportunity to manipulate the system for the benefit of himself and his buddies, and acted accordingly. In many of the cases that resulted in written grievances that went on to be dismissed, any competent shop steward would have resolved the matter verbally on the spot. Instead of fulfilling his duty to attempt to resolve issues verbally, Hopkins encouraged his fellow Wolfpack members to immediately file written grievances, which followed the strategy of building a case against Costello.

As a benefit of the mechanic position, Hopkins was allowed to fix his own and his family's vehicles in the city garage, another situation of which he took complete advantage. It was not a case where John objected to the vehicle of a DPW employee or family member being repaired in the city garage. Such is the way of the world, and Costello was not so rigid as to fail to recognize such realities. Hopkins had even performed minor repairs on Costello's son's car. However, the perk was taken to ridiculous extremes, turning it into what amounted to a side business. Repeatedly, when Costello would enter the DPW garage, he discovered Hopkins hard at work on a different private vehicle. Allowing the necessary work, for which he was being paid, to pile up, Hopkins spent much of his time running his repair shop on city time. As the union steward, one of Hopkins' chief complaints about Costello was the fact that he was seeking to privatize some of the DPW functions, such as lawn cutting and irrigation systems. This did not stop Hopkins, however, from repairing the commercial vehicles and equipment of those very same private contractors in the city garage.

Not only was the city losing money by paying Hopkins to operate an auto repair shop on the taxpayers' dollar, but the city vehicles and machinery were also being neglected, resulting in greater expense and difficulty completing necessary tasks. Costello recognized this dual problem in the city garage and took various steps to attempt to curtail Hopkins' behavior. He forbid Hopkins from working on any private vehicles outside of his immediate family, an edict that had about as much effect as forbidding the wind to blow. Hopkins received many memos from Costello criticizing his productivity in the auto shop and was verbally reprimanded as well, but the situation did not improve. Eventually, John took the drastic step of transferring Hopkins from the auto garage to the Street Dept.

Predictably enough, Hopkins immediately responded by killing more trees, filing a grievance claiming that he was taken out of his job description with the purpose of harassing the Union's steward. Costello countered that the transfer had nothing to do with Hopkins' position as shop steward, instead citing his continued lack of production and refusal to comply with DPW policies regarding utilization of city resources for personal gain. The matter went before City Manager Ciccarone, who settled the dispute in an expensive and somewhat puzzling manner. Ciccarone told Costello that he had settled the grievance to everyone's satisfaction, then revealed terms that flew in the face of the purpose of the transfer. He assured John that Hopkins still had to accept the transfer from the garage to the Street Dept, but as a concession, was to be promoted to Senior Foreman and given a three thousand dollar pay raise. Costello questioned what kind of message it would send to the rest of the DPW to reward a lack of production and defiance of the rules with a promotion and raise, and pointed out that in any other business, such a philosophy would surely lead to bankruptcy.

Despite the promotion and raise, Hopkins continued to seek to undermine Costello at every turn, even using his position in the Street Dept to spread anti-Costello propaganda. Shortly after the transfer, Costello received a call from an upset resident claiming that they had been taunted by Hopkins, who informed the resident that they were going to receive a summons for their trash. The resident told John that Hopkins had told them of the impending ticket not in an informative way, but in a way calculated to agitate the resident against Costello and his programs.

Hopkins also served to set a fine example to the men whom he represented, by constantly abusing the sick leave system. After several incidents of questionable absenteeism, Hopkins suddenly found himself held accountable, and did not react well at all. The occasion arrived on a morning when, as was his habit, Hopkins had simply not shown up nor bothered to call in. Costello phoned Hopkins' home to inquire as to the reason for his absence and received no answer. After further attempts to contact Hopkins failed, Costello actually became concerned. He asked Fred Hopkins, Mike's brother, who was also employed at DPW, to visit his brother's home and make sure there was no real problem. Fred pounded on his brother's door but still received no answer, which, considering the fact that

Mike Hopkins is morbidly obese and by no means the picture of health, caused him great worry. When he reported his findings back to the DPW office, Costello felt he had no alternative but to alert the police that there was the possibility of a genuine problem at Hopkins' home. John suggested that if the police felt the need to break into Hopkins' house, or perhaps remove a wall to get him out, they should go ahead and he would have the DPW make any necessary repairs. Fortunately, it all ended up as a false alarm, as Hopkins immediately answered the door once the police showed up. It turns out he was simply ignoring the phone and door in order to avoid having to deal with inquiries regarding his absence from work. Of course, Hopkins chose not to recognize John's sincere concern as such and the incident only served to further incense the union shop steward and his Wolfpack cronies.

And when speaking of cronies, no list can be complete without the inclusion of Ken Miller. Miller's relationship with Costello began on shaky ground and never really improved. When John first took over the position as Director of DPW, he discovered that Miller had no driver's license. This can be decidedly inconvenient when one's job title happens to contain the word "Driver". However, Miller had found a way around this inconvenience. He was simply driven around to his work assignments by a summer helper, who probably had not suspected when he applied for a job at DPW that he would actually be employed as a chauffeur. Costello was not pleased with this arrangement, but since it had existed before his hiring, he was prepared to tolerate the situation until Miller regained his driving privilege. To Miller, the mere fact that John disapproved of his being ferried around the island at city expense was enough to categorize Costello as the enemy.

Miller also harbored ill feelings over his removal from the irrigation installation crew. He did not see any potential for conflict in his spending the day in a city truck full of expensive irrigation materials while at the same time operating a private sprinkler and irrigation business. As far as he was concerned, the transfer was harassment, although he never did produce a plausible reason for which Costello might feel the need to torment him. He was transferred to the Water & Sewer Department, but after two weeks, supervisor Carmen Danunzio complained to Costello that Miller was disruptive and unproductive, and that he wished Miller to be transferred back out of his department.

So paranoid was Miller that he viewed even praise with suspicion and disdain. Although Costello had actually placed a few memos in his personnel file praising his performance, Miller remained convinced the praise was insincere, and maintained that John had some sinister ulterior motive in documenting his satisfaction on those occasions. Lest the impression be created that Costello stood alone as Miller's sole detractor, it should be pointed out that Miller's work performance was also monitored and criticized by Ernie Purdy and Carmen Danunzio

In September of 1997, Gibson, Miller and Hopkins worked overtime on a Friday night, utilizing a DPW pickup truck in the course of the job. By all accounts, the truck was in normal condition when the three took it out of the DPW yard. On Monday morning, it was brought to Costello's attention that the truck that had been used Friday night had somehow suffered severe damage to the driver's side door. Since the three Wolfpack members were the last people to have used the truck, naturally John sought to question them regarding the damage to the vehicle. He wanted to know how it happened and why it had not been reported immediately, and asked Ernie Purdy to make inquiries. Of course, to the Wolfpack, this constituted harassment and instantly provided another excuse to file frivolous grievances and distract everyone from the issue at hand, i.e. their irresponsibility.

Another grudge to which Miller bitterly clung was his resentment over not being assigned to spray pesticides and herbicides. Such duties require special licensing which is paid for by the city and although several DPW employees were certified to handle the poisonous chemicals, Miller had claimed the job as "his". In the reorganization of the department, this task fell to another employee and Miller felt wronged when informed that DPW would no longer require him to renew his license. This task was not tied to his irrigation duties of the same period, which he also saw as "his", nevertheless Miller insisted on renewing his license and filed a grievance when the city refused to pay. After the city reluctantly agreed to reimburse Miller for the renewal fee of $100, it was assumed that the issue was settled. Incredibly enough, when license renewal time came back around, Miller once again renewed his license without authorization and insisted that the city again reimburse him for the cost. Stretching the limits of believability even further, he filed another grievance when the city balked, and eventually got his money after signing an agreement that he would receive no further payment. Interestingly, once it had been made clear that the city would no longer pay, it became far less of a priority to Miller that his license be renewed, and he allowed it to lapse.

True to previously observed Wolfpack modus operandi, Miller had a significant history of sick leave abuse. City Manager Ciccarone performed an audit of sick time taken by all municipal employees, and Miller was determined to be one of the most serious transgressors. He seemed to have great difficulty grasping the concept that paid sick days were for actual situations in which an individual was sick, and that the money for those paid days off came out of the pockets of the taxpayers of Brigantine, one of whom Miller was not. Upon further investigation, it was found that an unusually high percentage of his sick days occurred on Fridays or Mondays. In 1995, Miller missed, and was paid for, no less than ten days that also happened to be just before or after the weekend. In 1996, it was nine, and in 1997, it was back up to ten. Sometimes, an even more extended weekend became necessary, and Miller would find himself compelled to take off either Thursday and Friday or Monday and Tuesday. Why not, when the city is footing the bill?

Unlike the rest of his buddies, though, Miller was not one to simply stay home without calling in. On the contrary, Miller was a master of the semi-plausible excuse. Once he called in to the DPW office and stated that his grandfather died, and then disappeared for four days. Upon his return, he was informed that the city's death benefit policy required that he provide a copy of the death certificate in order to be paid for the missed time. Miller responded by filing a Worker's Compensation claim that very day for a "sprained back" and going out on disability. While convalescing from his debilitating injury, Miller was routinely spotted cavorting in the surf and was rarely seen without his kayak loaded in the back of his truck, although he resides twenty miles away from the ocean, in Galloway. Weeks later, after repeated reminders, he managed to produce a reasonable facsimile of a death certificate, and the matter was mercifully dropped.

On another occasion, Miller called in and left a vague message stating that he had a sewer problem in his house and could not come to work. Costello attempted to return his call, but got no answer. He called once or twice more that morning, hoping to find out the scope of Miller's sewer problem and see how long it might keep him out of work, but still received no response or return call. As a last ditch effort, John called the DPW in Galloway and asked if they had received a service call for a sewer problem at Miller's home. Unbeknownst to Costello, and certainly not at his behest, the Galloway DPW extended the professional courtesy of visiting Miller's house and inquiring if he had a sewer problem with which he needed assistance. A flustered Miller declined their help and complained to his shop steward that he was being harassed, but did not file a grievance. Instead, he consulted an attorney and filed a criminal complaint against Costello for harassment. According to the police report, the responding officer advised Miller that he did not feel John's actions constituted harassment, and suggested that Miller carefully consider filing such a report. The officer made sure to note on the report that Miller had been informed of the repercussions that could arise from filing a false complaint, and had Miller sign a statement acknowledging that he had been so advised.

Approximately a week later, to his surprise, Costello received a summons from the Galloway Police. The city attorney represented John in the case, but they never went to court since Miller withdrew the complaint after John threatened civil action. In one of the most ironic statements ever made, Miller said he filed the charges because, *"I was infuriated. He wasted my tax dollars to send somebody to my house. That's not Brigantine. That's MY tax dollars."* Apparently, Miller *is* indeed aware of the correlation between the cost of wasted DPW resources and taxpayer dollars. As demonstrated by his outrage when DPW resources were squandered in *his* town, the shoe rarely fits comfortably on the proverbial other foot. However, Miller certainly did not mind wasting over three thousand dollars of Brigantine taxpayers' money on the legal fees required to fend off his frivolous charges.

Last, in both order of mention and status within the Wolfpack, was Joe Lombardo, who served no observable function other than adding to their numbers. Large size and a tough-guy attitude had carried him all the way to the DPW and the bottom of the totem pole in the Wolfpack hierarchy. One must always set lofty goals, after all. To his credit, Lombardo does hold the somewhat dubious distinction of being the best-behaved member of the Wolfpack, but only because he lacked the initiative to get into much mischief on his own. Perhaps being the son of the longtime elementary school principal resulted in his possessing a bit more self-discipline than his compatriots.

At first, John reckoned Lombardo to be a reasonably competent employee. He did not seem to be a troublemaker himself, even though he hung around with three of the worst one could ever hope to meet. Lombardo also had the pesticide/herbicide license that Ken Miller made such an issue of, but did not complain as Miller did when other licensed employees performed those duties. He also was not enterprising enough to attempt the renewal fee scam himself, so Costello was willing to give him the benefit of the doubt, despite his questionable taste in friends. The problems began when John began to interfere with Lombardo's second income stream. It seems Lombardo operated a private concrete business on the side, and constantly received calls at the DPW facility regarding his business on city time. When Costello put a stop to the practice, Lombardo became embittered and joined in on the Wolfpack's shenanigans with a vengeance.

Despite the minimal proficiency at concrete work one would assume to exist in the owner of a masonry business, Lombardo made sure he exhibited no such skill on city time. Every time he was assigned concrete work for the city, the job was so poorly done that it had to be chopped out and redone. At first, John assumed it to be a simple case of incompetence, and thought that if he forced Lombardo to redo the jobs until they were satisfactory, the point would be made. It soon became apparent that the problem went beyond mere ineptitude. The subject actually became a joke among the men in the DPW shop, and Costello was finally forced to relent and stop assigning Lombardo concrete work.

When Costello took over as Director, he made a priority of safety in the DPW and initiated a comprehensive program designed to decrease workplace injuries and keep accidents to a minimum. For reasons known only to him, Lombardo objected to the newly instituted safety measures and refused to comply. He received many complaints regarding safety violations, and repeatedly defied any efforts to correct his behavior. One of the safety measures John brought back was the requirement that all DPW employees wear an orange safety vest while performing any task that exposed them to traffic or pedestrians. Presumably, Lombardo's fashion sense railed at the thought of donning such a hideous ensemble, as he made a practice of losing, forgetting or damaging his vest to avoid wearing it. Despite constant verbal reminders, as well as several written memos, Lombardo refused to wear his vest. He had suddenly become an expert on safety issues, and had decided on his own that wearing an orange shirt would be sufficient. When confronted, Lombardo claimed that he had been advised by the city's insurance carrier that the safety policy allowed for the wearing of an orange shirt in the place of recognized safety gear. Unfortunately, he could not seem to come up with a name for this possibly imaginary insurance agent. Putting aside for a moment his credibility, or lack thereof, the fact remains that regardless of the opinions of any insurance agent, whether real or fictitious, John Costello was the sole arbiter of DPW policy. As Director, the final word, indeed the *only* word, on employee attire was his. Mister Blackwell may have disapproved, but Mister Costello did not care.

In a much more serious and potentially dangerous violation of safety regulations, Lombardo almost paid a terrible price when he thoughtlessly attempted to clear clogged grass clippings from the jammed blade of a running lawnmower bare-handed. Such mistakes can exact a heavy toll in the form of missing fingers; fortunately for Lombardo's math skills, he was lucky enough to avoid being maimed. When the lunacy of such a careless practice was pointed out to him, Lombardo still failed to grasp the seriousness of the situation, causing John to suspect that he may have been under the influence.

Lombardo's main function within the Wolfpack seemed to be as the attack dog. On orders from the "brains" of the group, he intimidated and threatened any DPW employee perceived as friendly to Costello. This perception could be derived from any number of dastardly behaviors, such as being on speaking terms with Costello, refusing to join the Wolfpack's activities, or even just the desire to do a fair day's work. At one point, an employee named Robert Bell approached John and claimed that he had been threatened with physical violence by Lombardo. Bell said that he had been perceived as an ally of Costello, and that he had been ordered to stop speaking with John or he would suffer a beating at the hands of the Wolfpack's enforcer. John's immediate response was to recommend reporting the incident to the police, but Bell was very concerned with the possibility of retaliation and begged John not to make any official report. Reluctantly, Costello agreed, but extracted a promise from Bell that he would report any further threats or harassing activity. Unfortunately, the employee had been correct in his assessment of the situation, and he did suffer repercussions for taking his problems to management. Bell operated a lawn-cutting business on the side, and he complained to Costello that DPW employees had conspired to damage his equipment. One of Bell's customers witnessed a DPW part-time summer helper unhooking Bell's equipment trailer from his truck, so that when Bell drove away, the trailer would become detached and possibly roll into traffic. This time, Costello convinced Bell to pursue his complaint with the police, and it was discovered that several DPW employees had advised the summer helper that they would assist him in gaining full-time employment with the city if he damaged Bell's equipment. Throughout Costello's trouble with the Wolfpack, Bell was always very helpful in passing information regarding the Wolfpack's latest scheme, which enabled John to stay a step ahead of their intrigues.

A bully's true nature will eventually rise to the surface, and Lombardo's case was no exception. The big weightlifter thought he had found an easy target in co-worker J.J. DiMatteo, who was described by Ernie Purdy as "*small and sickly.*" DiMatteo complained that he had been harassed by Lombardo, and threatened to file charges with the police if the conduct continued. When he was questioned regarding the situation by the City Manager, Lombardo counter-claimed that the diminutive DiMatteo had frightened him by turning his harmless "ball busting" into an angry confrontation. No matter how small the victim, the first display of guts will invariably send the bully scurrying for the shadows. Eventually, no other employees except his friends in the Wolfpack would even work around him. When he was assigned to clear an overgrown lot with a weed-whacker, Lombardo complained to Costello that he should not have to perform the job alone. He felt he was being picked on, but John shared his reason for assigning him a solo task. "*I don't have a problem with you, Joe. No one wants to work with you, that's why you're here by yourself.*"

Another of Lombardo's complaints was that John would drive around the island, passing by job sites to observe progress. Such activity would seem to be expected of a supervisor, but Lombardo saw much darker motives at work. He claimed that Costello would "*stop and try to intimidate you.*" When pressed for details, however, Lombardo claimed, "*I can't really recall any specific details at this time.*"

Examined individually, the members of the Wolfpack lose the intimidating aura that comes with running in a pack, and instead present a picture of arrested adolescence and inept buffoonery. Unable even to properly perform their jobs at the DPW, one would hardly think them able to bring an administration to its knees. And in that assessment one would be correct. Their many complaints had little to no effect on John, who was an expert at dealing with recalcitrant workers from his years in construction. On its own, the Wolfpack was an annoying distraction, but certainly no more than that. Costello was more than equal to the challenge to his leadership presented by four misfits, and likened them more to McHale's Navy than a pack of wolves.

Lest the impression be created that Costello forced an innocent group of misfits to band together in an attempt at self-preservation, it is important to note that their group existed long before John took over at DPW. They had been confederates in the subversion of DPW for years, and had only recently had their improper conduct revealed by the intense scrutiny brought to bear by Costello. Neither should it be inferred that these four individuals were the only ones to ever require discipline. Other employees certainly had their fair share of problems, but nothing invested with the malice and sinister agenda of the Wolfpack. However, it is interesting to note that while Costello served as Director, none of the employees ever made any harassment claims against him except Wolfpack members.

For example, the aforementioned J.J. DiMatteo freely admitted that he received a memo from Costello counseling him to watch his speed in city vehicles. Such a memo would be good for at least three grievances and a criminal charge of harassment from the Wolfpack, but DiMatteo seemed to take it in stride, like a professional. When asked if he considered John's corrective measure to be harassment, Di Matteo replied, *"I wouldn't consider it harassment. He was doing his job."* DiMatteo also characterized Costello as a boss who offered both praise and criticism fairly. Not only did he understand the motivation behind John writing him the memo criticizing his speed, but he also confirmed that John was just as quick to offer praise when deserved. *"Absolutely. I have memos at home from him on a number of jobs I was involved with, telling me how good a job I did. He really appreciated it."*

It was not only the other employees who felt the wrath of the Wolfpack. As the supervisor in charge of seeing to it that Costello's directives were carried out, Ernie Purdy served as a lighting rod for workers' complaints, as well. When they were not busy threatening to cut his throat, the Wolfpack inundated Purdy with claims of harassment and improper treatment by Costello. Spending at least 75 per cent of his day in John's presence, Purdy would have been in the best position of all to observe this alleged harassment. Instead, Purdy swore that he never saw John harass anyone, and that he offered both praise and criticism when appropriate.

Despite all the complaints leveled by the Wolfpack, it seemed obvious to most that their claims were, in the words of Shakespeare, *"A great sound and fury, signifying nothing."* This view was born out by the fact that the Teamsters union never involved itself in the complaints. As long as John adhered to the Teamsters' Collective Bargaining Agreement with the city, the men had nothing to complain about, and the union told them so.

Unfortunately, John was not finished rocking the boat.

6

Why People Hate Unions

The employees of the Brigantine DPW are members of the Chauffeurs, Teamsters and Helpers Union Local 331, based in Pleasantville, NJ. With a territorial jurisdiction covering Atlantic and Cape May counties, the Teamsters represent all blue-collar municipal employees throughout the area, as well as limousine drivers and those casino employees fortunate enough to work in "union houses." At the time, local 331 was headed by President and CEO Joseph Yeoman.

As bargaining representative for the DPW employees, the Teamsters are responsible for negotiating contracts and working conditions for their members, and for resolving any labor disputes that might arise. Serving as Business Agent, the direct liaison between the city and the union, was David Tucker. Tucker was a union employee who represented the DPW workers in dealings and negotiations between DPW employees and the city. Additionally, a fund was set aside, at the expense of the taxpayers, to provide attorneys for any Teamster member who might wish to sue the city or even one of the very taxpayers who provided the funds.

With such arrogance-inducing contractual stipulations in place it is easy to understand why it was not long after John Costello took over the reins at the Brigantine DPW that friction began to develop between him and the union. One of John's first acts as the new Director was to cut the workforce, laying off several employees in an effort to increase efficiency. While the drop in membership, with its corresponding drop in dues payments, certainly did not please the union, Tucker was willing to acknowledge that Costello was within his rights to trim away some of the DPW deadwood. Much harder for the Teamsters to stomach was Costello's skill and determination at the negotiating table. Because of his long and successful career at the top levels of the construction industry, John had a plethora of practical experience with the inner workings and operations of organized labor unions and their negotiations. As a result, he turned out to be a much more tenacious negotiating opponent for the Teamsters, who were used to rolling over the former Director and virtually always having things their way. John had been on their side of the table and knew all the tricks of the trade, a fact that the Teamsters seemed to view as a betrayal of Costello's union roots.

Even then, the Teamsters were still prepared to peacefully coexist with Costello. When the Wolfpack first started up their shenanigans, the union refused to back their frivolous grievances and showed no interest in joining the anti-Costello crusade. It did not bother or surprise Tucker that John was irritating some known troublemakers with his new policies, and the union certainly was not going to back the men in frivolous grievances simply for the sake of solidarity. That would require a threat to something much more sacred to them than union brotherhood. It took a threat to the union's finances. John had already cut the DPW staff down to 25 employees from 36, which directly affected union membership. Since his organizational efforts allowed the DPW to operate with an increase of efficiency even though there was a decrease in manpower, the Teamsters did not have much of a case to argue against the reductions in force.

However, the union suddenly became much more interested in the Wolfpack's complaints once John began to look into the privatization of some of the services provided by public works employees as another cost-cutting measure. If Costello's efforts to streamline the department and turn some responsibilities over to private firms angered the union, then his ability to obtain documentation proving that privatization would be more efficient terrified them. The work order system Costello had implemented showed the costs that the taxpayers were incurring by having certain functions performed by DPW employees. Analysis showed that it would be much more cost efficient for the city to have some of the tasks performed by private contractors. With a private contractor, the city would simply pay a set fee for a particular service to be performed, instead of a lifetime of salary and benefits. The savings in pension, health and retirement benefits alone would be huge. In reducing the number of employees and hiring less expensive labor, the city not only saved money, but also had an easier time making up the budget for the following year.

John was not looking to cut the Teamsters completely out of the picture, but instead simply wanted to have them bid for the work like any other contractor. The union and its membership were adamantly against any such situation, even though many other towns use this system very successfully. They feared that privatization meant that some people would lose their jobs, which was not necessarily even true. If an existing DPW employee wished to stay on with the new contractor and continue performing a certain task to which they feel especially suited, in some cases that opportunity would be available to them. However, some of the DPW employees had become accustomed to the undemanding pace of municipal employment, and showed no sign of any ability to adjust to the demands of a competitive workplace. Perhaps they realized that they would have great difficulty surviving in the world of private enterprise, where a certain level of production is demanded, which would explain the vigor with which they fought against the concept of privatization.

After all, there are in this world those who, frankly, only the government can afford to employ, since any private businessman would be quickly driven to bankruptcy by their incompetence. Perhaps someday scientists will perform a study on how governmental jobs sometimes seem to fill a niche, by providing employment to the otherwise unemployable. One might suspect that some sort of municipal Darwinism would dictate that quality people would land these jobs by virtue of being better applicants, and that the unemployable would simply be unemployed. However, evidence seems to show that quite frequently, these positions are filled by social misfits with powerful relatives. It may be that an even more interesting study would be one focusing on the correlation between politicians and their genetic connections with the otherwise unemployable.

While the employees were horrified by the possibility of being thrust into the competitive working world, the union was more worried about the perceived threat to its income. Costello was looking into the privatization of trash collection on city cans, beach raking, lawn cutting and irrigation system installation, as well as most of the duties of the Water & Sewer Department. To the Teamsters, this meant a substantial reduction in dues paying members, which was patently unacceptable, despite the apparent logic inherent in Costello's proposals.

The union successfully fought off John's efforts to privatize the lawn cutting duties, even though he had an idea that might have been beneficial for the entire community. John developed a plan to divide the different DPW grass-cutting responsibilities into different categories, and then put each category up for bid to a different contractor. Brigantine then contained, and still does, a multitude of lawn-care companies, and Costello thought it might be good to support the island's economy by awarding city work to the best of the best. He reasoned that the city would retain tight control on the maintenance of its properties, since if a contractor failed to perform his duties, there would be six more waiting in the wings for the chance to pick up the contract. John even thought of allowing the contractors to post small, discreet signs proclaiming the name of the company responsible for the work in that particular section of town. Despite significant projected savings, the idea was flatly rejected because it would cost city employees jobs.

As hard as the union fought against it, some of the DPW services were eventually privatized, at great savings to the city. Trash collection had already been contracted to a private firm, which performed the duties much more efficiently, and at a much lower cost. Sprinkler and irrigation installation was also privatized, something for which Costello successfully lobbied after removing Ken Miller from the position. Once the new company was brought in, however, the union membership demonstrated that the matter was far from settled. Soon after the private contractor had installed a new sprinkler system in the grass median strip on Brigantine Blvd., the main road into town, a curious "accident" occurred. Ken Miller, Mike Hopkins and Joe Lombardo, while working on an assignment to plant and groom the center median strip island, rode a 2-ton tractor down the middle of the grass island and crushed the heads of every single sprinkler. The crushed sprinkler heads and ruined irrigation system had to be repaired at further taxpayer expense, but the culprits simply laughed it off, claiming it had simply been a "mistake." Costello was especially incensed at this occurrence, since Hopkins was the union shop steward, and his participation in such conduct implied the approval of the Teamsters local.

At first, Ciccarone encouraged Costello to look into privatizing some of the DPW functions, especially when there was credit to be taken for the savings to the taxpayers. However, when the acclaim for cutting costs died down, all that was left was the negative feelings of the union and the DPW employees, some of whom Ciccarone had personal relationships with. As soon as he began to feel that pressure, the slippery political operator quickly backed off his support of privatization.

The privatization issue actually became something of a political hot potato, since none of the island's politicians was eager to get involved on either side of the argument. On the one hand, there is the general political benefit one would expect from supporting a measure that would cut costs and presumably lower taxes. On the other hand, Brigantine is a small island. In many cases, DPW employees have these city jobs because of political connections. For City Council to make a decision that might eliminate some city jobs could turn a potentially unemployed city worker against their ward Councilman. This could prove costly to the party in terms of votes, considering that most of the DPW employees had plenty of friends and family on the island. With property values rising, more and more Brigantine real estate has been purchased as second homes by nonresidents, who pay high property taxes but have no vote. In terms of political realities, it is no surprise that Brigantine's politicians had no interest in displeasing potentially large blocks of voters just to save some wealthy shoobies some property taxes. Another political consideration was the fact that less DPW positions would mean less money budgeted to Brigantine by the state next year. In addition, a reduced number of city jobs equals less patronage to dispense for supporters, most of whom only act as such in exchange for the promise of future favors. As a result, John found himself in a position of trying to do the right thing for the taxpayers, but without the support of the City Manager or most of its elected officials.

From this point on, John found himself in an adversarial relationship with the union that constantly strained the boundaries of cordiality. On one occasion, Teamsters President Joseph Yeoman attended a meeting with Costello and Cicca-rone and attempted to intimidate and coerce the city representatives into compliance by throwing a temper tantrum replete with profanities and veiled threats. John felt that Yeoman's behavior was completely outrageous by any professional standards and walked out of the meeting, which he now suspects was Yeoman's objective all along. By driving John out of the meeting, the union no longer had to deal with him. After that day, the Teamsters developed a new strategy of refusing to meet with Costello. They also suddenly became adamant that John be removed from the negotiation process. The union justified its stance by complaining that final authority for binding agreements did not rest with Costello. Since John reported to Ciccarone, the Teamsters claimed that by being forced to meet with a "middleman", they were being disrespected. Thenceforth, they wished to meet only with Ciccarone, even though the Collective Bargaining Agreement (CBA) specifically stated that the Superintendent of Public Works was to be the city's representative in any negotiations concerning the DPW.

When the city persisted in presenting John as the contract negotiator, further steps were taken to discourage his participation. In 1997, the Teamsters and Costello sat down for contract renegotiations, but for some reason, the Teamsters did not have their copy of the City's contract proposal. John knew that he had personally furnished a copy well in advance to Mike Hopkins, but Teamster negotiator Tucker claimed that he had not seen the proposal. When a copy was produced for him, Tucker had to retire to a separate room to read it over before negotiations could resume. During the wait, John curiously asked Hopkins why he had not furnished the copy of the proposal to his union as he was supposed to, to which Hopkins replied *"I wiped my ass with it."* When informed of the conduct of his on the job representative, Tucker implied that such comments were not at all unusual during Teamster negotiations.

In another effort to improve relations with the union, John wrote Tucker a letter proposing that the two of them attend a monthly meeting or luncheon where they could talk over issues and stay in close communication, but Tucker refused. He contemptuously declared, *"I would never have lunch with an employee"* and again insisted on dealing only with Ciccarone. According to Tucker's own notes, at one meeting John pleaded with the union that he *"wanted communication, not legal battles"*, and that he was *"willing to work"* to sort out any problems that might exist. Tucker's notes do not reflect his reasons for refusing Costello's entreaties, but it is no great leap to surmise that the Teamsters just wanted someone easier to negotiate with. John could not be cajoled or intimidated like Ciccarone, and as a result, the union wanted to negotiate with the City Manager alone. According to Tucker's notes of a discussion with Ciccarone, Yeoman complained that the city was trying to save too much money, something for which Ciccarone actually *apologized.*

John repeatedly offered to meet with the Teamsters to attempt to iron things out, but instead the union started a campaign to have him removed as Director of Public Works. The started by encouraging the filing of frivolous grievances and criminal complaints, and by supporting the Wolfpack in their strategy of disrupting the operations of the DPW.
The plan was to bury Costello in an avalanche of grievances. As one employee said, *"There was always somebody filing a grievance about something, if the wind blew the wrong way. That's how bad it was. Everybody was always filing grievances. What they were about I couldn't tell you."*

For the most part, the grievances concentrated mostly on complaints regarding work assignments. A total of six written grievances were filed against Costello in

relation to work assignments, and not surprisingly, every one of those six grievances was filed by a Wolfpack member. Unhappy with the fact that John had
control of the job assignments, the Wolfpack felt that work should be assigned
based on seniority. However, the union's collective bargaining agreement plainly
states that seniority was relevant only with respect to layoffs and vacation. It was
at John's sole discretion to give virtually any assignment to a Laborer/Operator/
Driver, which was the job title held by all DPW employees. Job assignments were
a management prerogative, since the city had strong management rights clauses
in the CBA that they had refused to modify over the years, and John had full
authority to assign work to DPW employees without consideration of the length
of time the worker had been employed there. Regardless of the terms of the CBA,
the Wolfpack repeatedly filed grievances against Costello and insisted that they
should receive favorable assignments because of their seniority. Instead, John
handed out job assignments based on productivity and suitability to the task at
hand. This commonly resulted in the Wolfpack members receiving assignments
they saw as less than desirable, since their productivity level was usually among
the lowest in the department.

As one of his highest priorities, John kept a close eye on departmental productivity, and took steps to remedy any problems that stood in the way of completing a
job in an efficient and expeditious manner. For example, there were two lawn
cutting crews operating on the island on any given day. Crew One was made up
of Bobby Gibson, Joe Lombardo and another anonymous misfit. Crew Two consisted of two normal full time employees and a seasonal helper. On one beautiful
spring day, Costello conducted a comparative review of the productivity of the
two lawn crews and found an alarming disparity in production levels.

On May 14, John sent a memo to Ernie Purdy and copied Ciccarone, shop steward Hopkins and the Teamsters union. The memo itemized the amount of lawn
cut by each crew and added up the square footage involved in each parcel of land.
Crew One, consisting of Gibson, Lombardo and another employee, ended with a
total of 40,743 square feet of lawn cut that day, between three full time employees. Crew Two ended the day with a total of 139,487 square feet of lawn cut,
between two full time employees and a teenage summer helper.

Because of production levels such as these, John felt compelled to remove the
Wolfpack members from tasks requiring speed or production, and instead
assigned them jobs at which he felt they might have more success. The Wolfpack

members claimed that they were embarrassed and degraded by some of these tasks, such as scraping weeds from gutters, sweeping the street or cleaning litter from the traffic island on the main street. John expressed surprise at the ingratitude exhibited by the Wolfpack, when he was simply trying to find duties that were suited to their special abilities.

The union also overlooked Mike Hopkins' abuse of the grievance process by allowing him to circumvent the union's agreement with the city. Article six, section B of the CBA lays out a Preliminary Informal Procedure, which requires the grieving party to orally present their problem on an informal basis to their shop steward. The steward must then determine the legitimacy of the complaint and decide on one of two possible courses of action. Most times a competent shop steward, having an enhanced understanding of the Collective Bargaining Agreement, will inform the employee that the grievance is not meritorious. In the event the grievance is found by the steward to be legitimate, he will then orally present the issue to the appropriate supervisor on an informal basis, and attempt to resolve the dispute. Either way, the written grievance procedure is not supposed to begin until the informal process has at least been attempted. Hopkins never attempted to resolve anything informally, and instead immediately took any issue directly to the formal, written stage in an effort to pile up complaints against Costello. The union never instructed Hopkins to do otherwise, even though Tucker expressed surprise at the unreasonably high number of written grievances coming in from one small community. Additionally, Costello found that many of the grievances against him by the Wolfpack had been filed directly with the City Manager, without John even receiving a copy. This was in direct violation of the grievance procedure outlined in the CBA, which called for proper chain of command to be followed, and for all involved parties to receive a copy of any grievance in which they are involved. These underhanded tactics did not help, however, since most often, these grievances were vague and unsupported, and the union abandoned the charges without a hearing. Further grievances regarding John checking up on employees' sick leave excuses were also dismissed, because according to the language of the CBA, he had every right to do it.

Finally, once the matter had been permitted to generate several frivolous grievances, David Tucker acknowledged that nothing in the Collective Bargaining Agreement obligated John to assign work by seniority. Since all the grievances filed against Costello were in regards to job assignments, the union was forced to dismiss the complaints. However, the true purpose behind the filings had been served. The foundation was laid for more serious charges, alleging that Costello was harassing his men.

Finally, once the union felt it had established enough of a pattern; Teamsters local 331 filed a complaint with the Public Employment Relations Commission (PERC) that alleged only "discrimination". The complaint was purportedly signed by Yeoman, but it was later revealed that Tucker had filled out the form and signed Yeoman's name. It is unknown if Yeoman was in fact aware of this filing. Not surprisingly, PERC contacted the union advising that the unfair labor practice charge it had filed was incomplete and needed to be amended to provide detail or it would be dismissed. Key details, such as the date of the alleged discrimination, or the precise section of the agreement that they claimed had been violated, were missing from the complaint. These charges had potentially serious consequences, and PERC could not pursue a claim that had not even been filled out completely. The complaint was filed in October of 1997. PERC sent the first letter requesting more details in November. They sent another letter in December, informing the union that if they did not respond with an amended complaint that complied with the requirements of the statute, the complaint would be deemed abandoned. The Teamsters never replied, and PERC dropped the complaint.

Obviously, the union did not intend to actually pursue any legitimate claim with PERC, instead simply being satisfied with the fact that they had managed to place another stain on John's record. The DPW employees, beginning to feel a bit lost in the shuffle, were not satisfied. They expected immediate action to be taken against Costello, and expressed dissatisfaction with Tucker's efforts on their behalf. During a meeting between Tucker and the Wolfpack members at the DPW shop, the members expressed anger at the union and said, *"Something more has to be done."*

Although he did not really believe it, Tucker attempted to reassure them that Costello was on his way out, replying, *"We're working on it."*

7

Ten Pounds in a Five-Pound Bag

As if the internal labor problems in the department were not enough, Costello was also forced to contend with the persistent meddling of insidious outside forces. Fourth Ward Councilman James Frugoli emerged as another major impediment to John's efforts to operate the DPW in an efficient manner, and, unlike the Wolfpack, proved to be a most cunning adversary.

James Frugoli had moved to Brigantine in 1970, but never entered the political arena until he retired in 1993 from a career as an insurance salesman. By then both of his sons were already deeply entrenched in strong municipal jobs: one as a police officer, the other as a firefighter, and their family name had become well known around town. Therefore, when John Costello approached him in May of 1993 with an offer to take over the fourth ward Council seat vacated by Mike Hilferty, Frugoli jumped at the chance. He finished out the remainder of Hilferty's term, then retained his office with a victory over the Democratic candidate in the following November's elections. Already beginning to believe his own hype, Frugoli, still a slick salesman despite his paunch and hound-dog jowls imagined himself to be the newly crowned political powerhouse on the island. He began to refer to the fourth ward as "Outpost Four", even going so far as to christen his new boat with the same name.

Being on the City Council had inflated his ego to the point where Frugoli began to fancy himself something of a Godfather to his ward. He enjoyed having residents come scraping before him to kiss his ring and beg for favors. With a pontifical wave of his hand, he would grant the request, and then expect the DPW to drop everything and get right on his task. After all, for what other purpose did the department exist than to make the Godfather look good to his constituents? Under the administration of former Superintendent Gibson, such an arrangement was easily achieved. After all, Frugoli had served as Gibson's insurance agent for 30 years before he had retired, so it was a simple matter of asking a favor of a friend. Likewise, when Gibson retired from the DPW, Frugoli felt no conflict in paying his good friend back for all his help by voting for a Lakes-owned firm to receive the lucrative water-consulting contract for Brigantine, the results of which have already been mentioned.

Under the administration of John Costello, the situation was entirely different. According to the Faulkner Act, *"Council members are strictly prohibited from (1) seeking to influence in any way the performance of the official acts of the Manager or any other city officer, (2) from interfering in any way with the performance by such officers of their duties and (3) from giving orders to any subordinates of the manager, either publicly or privately."* Plainly put, Frugoli was prohibited by law from giving any direct orders to the Director of the DPW or any DPW employees. Costello repeatedly advised Frugoli of the appropriate chain of command, which demanded that Council members submit any work requests to the City Manager. Of course, this is not to say that other Council members did not occasionally come to John with an unofficial request that he take care of a particular situation with haste. When circumstances dictated immediate action, John was able to act on an emergency request, but for the most part, Council members followed the official procedure. Unfortunately, the Commander of Outpost Four felt himself to be above such annoyances and instead made it his practice to simply barge right into Costello's office and demand that a given task be performed immediately in his ward.

Many times, these projects involved a significant amount of man-hours, required the use of heavy equipment, and constituted a considerable expenditure of resources. Frugoli routinely demanded that large projects, such as curb and street repairs, large cleanups, sod placement, installation of sprinkler systems, creating new dirt roads and placing beach barriers, be performed immediately, instead of following the chain of command and submitting an official request. The word request was not in Frugoli's vocabulary, however. He was always quite adamant and forceful when he made these demands, using phrasing like, *"I want it done"*, *"Take care of this right away"*, and *"Just do it."*

The problem was that John had a schedule of work orders and could not disrupt the entire operation merely to immediately satisfy Frugoli's need to look important to his constituents. It was certainly not a case in which Costello did not want to perform the tasks in Frugoli's ward. It was simply that John had reduced the

DPW work force, and for the department to be able to operate efficiently, it had to run in an organized fashion. Disrupting the program would cause the DPW to stop functioning properly. About those problems, Frugoli could not have cared less, viewing the DPW as nothing more than a political tool to be utilized for maximum benefit. He insisted that his ward receive top priority over projects in any other wards, effectively diverting taxpayer resources directly into Frugoli's re-election campaign on no better authority than his own.

John attempted to point out the potential for conflict and abuse if the DPW was permitted to be used in such a way, refusing to perform any project that involved a considerable amount of money without first obtaining official approval. However, Frugoli was not interested in such niceties, becoming angry and implying dire consequences if he was not satisfied. Forgetting who had put him in his lofty position in the first place, Frugoli cautioned Costello to consider the ramifications of his continued refusals to obey, reminding John to know his place by telling him, "...*the tail don't wag the dog!*"

In an attempt to prevent an already uncomfortable situation from growing even worse, John met with City Manager Tom Ciccarone and asked him to intercede with Frugoli on his behalf. However, Ciccarone and Frugoli were personal friends, and Costello's pleas were ignored. The City Manager refused to take the matter seriously and provided no relief. Ironically, Ciccarone finally did involve himself, but with an unexpected twist. On this occasion, Costello had relented under Frugoli's constant badgering and agreed to install a sprinkler system and new sod in the grass median strip dividing the street on which Frugoli just happens to live. Absurdly enough, upon completion of the project, John was verbally reprimanded by Ciccarone for performing the work on Frugoli's orders and not awaiting official approval!

With Frugoli's demands now causing a conflict between himself and his boss, John finally grew exasperated with the whole situation and clearly informed the Councilman that no more unofficial requests would be entertained. John also pointed out to Frugoli that the Faulkner Act, Brigantine's new form of government, precluded a Council member from directing any city employee, particularly in the field. This made Frugoli's actions not only inappropriate but also technically illegal. Frugoli's response to this was to violate Faulkner even further by bringing his demands directly to Costello's subordinates, contravening John's orders and pressuring the employees to keep quiet about it. One does not have to strain to imagine how intimidated the poor guy in the field must have felt when the big, bad Councilman came blustering along, barking orders and throwing around his not-inconsiderable weight. One might imagine an employee would feel that a Councilman outranks a Director of Public Works, and feel obligated to comply. As a result, John began to find employees had abandoned assigned tasks in favor of some other job for which a work order had not yet even been generated. Upon questioning the employee, he was repeatedly told that Frugoli had come along and directed them to do so. This effectively undermined Costello's authority and placed undue stress upon the employees of the department. Several employees complained to John about feeling "caught in the middle" between Costello and Frugoli, and said they felt afraid for their jobs if they disobeyed the Councilman. Ernie Purdy, who Frugoli approached most often, felt especially uncomfortable, since he worked closely with John, but also found himself to be a resident of "Outpost Four". Purdy was repeatedly put in the position of having to fend off Frugoli's advances, imploring him to disobey Costello and attend to some project that might win him a few more votes.

At the root of most of the antagonism between Frugoli and Costello seemed to be a simple case of petty jealousy. The Councilman envied John because he *was* the political godfather that Frugoli could only aspire to be. Incapable of gratitude toward the very person who had put him in the position he enjoys so much, Frugoli bitterly resented the fact that although John was a mere department head, he still had enough political clout to defy a Council member. Even worse, Frugoli knew that one of his biggest public relations coups came as a direct result of Costello, a secret he only reluctantly revealed much later. It seems that Harbor View Villas, a condominium development in the fourth ward, had developed an unusually bad problem with litter and debris on the streets. Not normally an area that received much attention from Frugoli, the development was scoured from end to end while the Councilman pompously supervised and pressed flesh with the grateful residents. The following week, a letter was printed in the local newspaper lauding Frugoli for taking care of the problem in such an efficient manner, and for being so attentive to the needs of his ward. Long after he had wrung as much political capital as possible from the situation, Frugoli later grudgingly admitted, *"It was John's idea to get the kids that were working in the summer to come down and clean the streets because of the debris and the nonsense that was going on in the neighborhood. He came to me and said we're going to do a clean-up project down there and you'll take credit for it."*

However, no matter how John tried to work along with Frugoli, nothing he did was ever enough. Frugoli continually insisted on special treatment. While Costello cited numerous instances of inappropriate behavior, no other situation exemplifies the political avarice of Councilman Frugoli better than the story of Coquille Beach.

Coquille Beach is the name of a beautiful two hundred-unit beachfront condominium development in Frugoli's fiefdom of the fourth ward. Residents of Coquille Beach were treated to a picturesque backdoor view of the sand dunes and the ocean beyond. Directly behind the development, at the foot of the dunes, lay a walking path no wider than six to eight feet. Somewhat overgrown with weeds and vegetation, the path sat on the edge of the sand dunes, just steps from the back doors of the Coquille Beach residents.

The Coquille Beach condominium development, behind which Councilman Frugoli insisted on creating a road on protected wetlands.

Those residents, and the hundreds of votes they represented, had called a meeting in order to complain to Frugoli about the ocean flooding from which they suffered any time the island was hit by a severe storm. Never one to miss a chance to curry favor, Frugoli's solution was to immediately propose that the city pay to fill in, widen and raise the elevation of this path, essentially creating a road behind the condominiums, running parallel to the beach. Despite the fact that nobody knew whether the path was city-owned or privately owned by the condominium development, Frugoli wanted to perform the task at city expense. Since the path is not shown on the city's beach access plan, it would seem clear that the path was not the responsibility of the city. Throughout John's tenure as Director of DPW, he never believed the path was on city property, and never directed any DPW employees to care for the path in any way. Regardless, Frugoli had taken a particular interest in this project, insisting that it be completed immediately. He was eager for the city to make yet another involuntary campaign contribution to his re-election fund.

Not long after the issue was first raised, the Councilman was nosing around the DPW yard one day and happened to notice a large pile of dirt that had been removed from the site of a sewer line break. The dirt was not what is termed "clean fill" since it contained fragments of broken sewer pipe, asphalt and other contaminants. It was being stored in the DPW yard for use in the event of a hurricane. Seizing his opportunity, Frugoli demanded that John utilize this dirt to build the road on the beach. Costello informed the councilman that such materials were hardly appropriate for use in the beach area. Up to this point, the request was not all that outrageous. It was inappropriate and selfish, but that was nothing out of the ordinary for Frugoli. The far worse offense was that he had technically broken the law in directing John to do the job, but again, this was all familiar territory. A more serious problem arose when Costello met with City Engineer Matthew Doran and advised him of Frugoli's request. Doran informed Costello that the area containing the path was considered wetlands, and therefore protected from any type of work being performed. When asked if the path behind Coquille Beach could be widened, Doran told John, "*...absolutely not. That's wetlands area, don't go in there. If you go in there, you're on your own.*"

The importance of the sand dunes cannot be overstated, especially to a barrier island like Brigantine, which is the reason for the strict protection afforded these locations by state and federal authorities. Not only do the dunes serve to protect the beach from massive erosion that can result from storms but they also provide

a habitat for protected species of plants and birds. When John informed the City
Engineer's office of Frugoli's request to use the contaminated dirt, Doran advised
Costello that he would not authorize the placement of recycled asphalt facing and
dirty fill on the beach or wetlands, and that to do so would be in violation of EPA
statutes. He further stated that even clean fill could not be placed on the beach
without Doran's recommendation, which would not be forthcoming without a
permit from the Department of Environmental Protection. Even if the city were
to receive a permit from the DEP, Doran stressed that the dirt Frugoli wanted to
use was absolutely out of the question for that area.

When informed of this development, Frugoli became incensed that Costello did
not simply obey his orders and had instead consulted Doran. He remained adamant that not only would the project go ahead, but also that the contaminated
dirt from the broken sewer line would indeed be used. Frugoli visited John's
office two or three more times to argue his case further, to no avail. Costello
advised Frugoli that he had a license to protect, and could not defy the City Engineer's recommendation. Each time he was refused Frugoli's displays of temper
and frustration grew more extravagant.

According to Doran, he met with Frugoli regarding this project and told the
Councilman clearly that a letter of authorization from the DEP would be necessary before any work could be done in the area of the path. Frugoli, not surprisingly, denies any memory of such a conversation.

Frugoli's response was to continue to attempt to cajole Costello into committing
this crime, reasoning, *"Nobody will know."* John continued to stand firm in his
refusals, all the while appealing to the City Manager for assistance in dealing with
the determined councilman. When Frugoli's demands subsided, John figured he
had finally been granted some relief. Unfortunately, this assumption proved to be
incorrect, as Frugoli was simply biding his time. More than a month later, John
happened to notice a few city trucks in the DPW yard being loaded with dirt.
Reasonably sure that he had not assigned any earth moving tasks that day, John
consulted Ernie Purdy and was informed that Frugoli had issued orders to have
the dirt taken from the DPW yard and dumped on the path at Coquille Beach.
Incensed, Costello ordered Purdy to dump the dirt back in the yard and return
the trucks to the garage. John was already annoyed with the fact that Frugoli had
attempted to sneak behind his back to do something that he knew perfectly well
was not permitted. However, he was even more upset that Frugoli had once again

undermined his authority by issuing orders directly to John's subordinates, yet another flagrant violation of the Faulkner Act. Ernie Purdy complained of once again having been put in the middle of conflict, and rightly expected protection from such treatment. When informed of this latest obstruction to his plans, Frugoli confronted Costello at the DPW office and was furious that John had once again stopped the project from going forward. He threw a threatening and abusive temper tantrum with displays of anger and rage so impressive that Costello was actually moved to make a written note of Frugoli's condition. The Councilman relented on the road subject for a few weeks, but eventually he found a way to get what he wanted.

Another anecdote that even more clearly illustrates the perfidy of the rotund Councilman from the fourth ward was his continual conflict with Costello regarding municipal summonses issued for violations in his ward.

As part of the effort to clean up the island, the city had instituted, at Costello's urging, a program whereby residents who improperly disposed of trash would be ticketed and fined. This program served to greatly reduce the refuse and litter problems, but unfortunately also led to hard feelings among some residents who felt that they should be above such legalities. Frugoli the Fixer, once again seeking to throw his estimable weight around, approached John, complaining that friends of his had received summonses and he had promised to get the tickets, *"taken care of."* He told Costello, *"I want you to straighten this out. I told the guy I would help him with this ticket."*

John refused to cooperate and advised Frugoli that once the ticket was written, it had to stand. The person would have to either pay the fine or show up in court to contest the charge, which was a rare occurrence. When John went on to suggest that Frugoli had broken the law simply by asking for such a favor, the Councilman became very angry and belligerent, blustering once again that *"the tail doesn't wag the dog"*. John countered by advising Frugoli that if he wanted to be such a big deal in the eyes of his constituents, he ought to simply pay the ticket for the resident and just tell them he'd had the ticket fixed. Of course, such a solution would require a long reach into his pocket by the notoriously short-armed Councilman, so that suggestion was of no use to Frugoli.

Once again, time passed and Frugoli seemed to relent. However, over time, John gradually began to notice that the city had been losing some of the cases in court, whereas they had formerly won practically every one. He checked into the situation further and discovered that some tickets had been dismissed once they reached court, and that the evidence relating to other cases was suddenly disappearing, causing the ticket to be vacated by the court. Aside from himself, John knew that the only people with the authority to dismiss a trash summons were Ernie Purdy, his assistant, and Kelly Wilson, his secretary. He found that both had been pressured by Frugoli to dismiss tickets or misplace evidence, and to conceal the fact from Costello. Purdy told John that he felt threatened by Frugoli and feared the ramifications on his career if he refused to comply with the Councilman's orders. Ernie again expressed regret at being placed in the middle of the situation, as did John's secretary, but both insisted that they had been made to feel as though their jobs were at stake.

John explained that he understood their position, and that he would do his best to prevent further occurrences, but he stressed to both that under no circumstances were any tickets to be dismissed without his knowledge, and that to do otherwise was a very serious violation of the law. In an effort to nip the problem in the bud, Costello also wrote a letter to the Court Administrator, with a copy to Ciccarone, emphasizing that no ticket issued by the DPW was to be dismissed for any reason without John's approval. Despite all John's efforts, tickets continued to be mysteriously dismissed, forcing him to be increasingly vigilant.

After a period where John was forced to attend every session of court in an effort to catch someone dismissing a ticket, he finally managed to discourage Frugoli from attempting to circumvent the law. Or so he thought. Instead, as John found out, Frugoli had simply changed strategies. This became obvious when Costello was summoned to Ciccarone's office and informed that there were too many tickets being issued. Ciccarone told John that the summonses had become a political issue; one that some Council members feared might cost them votes. Residents were starting to complain about receiving the tickets, and expected help from their respective ward leaders. With Costello unwilling to play ball, residents were beginning to express dissatisfaction with the inability of their Council members to keep the Director of Public Works under control.

As a solution, the City Manager directed John to "cut back" on the trash summonses, in other words telling him to turn a blind eye to most of the ordinance violations in town. Ciccarone explained that he did not want John to stop writing tickets altogether, just to cut back and be mindful to who tickets were issued. Of course, Frugoli denies ever asking Costello to fix any tickets, expressing shock at the very suggestion. When cornered, however, he will admit to having been investigated in the past by both the County Prosecutor and the State's Attorney General for attempting to fix traffic tickets. No charges were filed, and the simple fact that one has been accused of a misdeed in the past does not mean that present accusations of the same misdeed are necessarily true. In a completely unrelated story, fire has been discovered by scientists to be the usual source of smoke.

Beset from within and without by insurrection, incompetence and interference, John continued in his attempts to keep the DPW running efficiently. Hoping for some assistance with his problems regarding both Councilman Frugoli and the Wolfpack, Costello turned to the man who had hired him, the City Manager.

However, John had one more I-word to learn.

Indifference.

8

Hail to Little Caesar

Throughout his conflicts with both the Wolfpack and Councilman Frugoli, there was one man to whom John should have been able to turn for relief. That man was his direct supervisor, City Manager Tom Ciccarone. Known informally in Brigantine's political circles as "Chick", Ciccarone stood only five foot seven inches tall and was known around town to suffer from a bit of a Napoleonic Complex. Referred to behind his back by the City Hall secretaries as "Little Caesar", Chick often let his insecurities cloud his judgment, sometimes making arbitrary decisions seemingly for the sheer sake of demonstrating his power. Ciccarone was not only in a position to resolve both of Costello's problems, but indeed, had a duty to do so. Instead, the City Manager chose to remain uninvolved, at least officially.

A slick political operative with long experience in the political trenches, Ciccarone was on the personal staff of Michael Matthews, the former Mayor of Atlantic City who was removed from office and imprisoned for corruption in 1984. Not surprisingly, Chick walked away from the situation unscathed. He went on to hold a municipal administration position in the seaside town of Avalon, NJ, but did not remain at that post for long. By 1991, Ciccarone had taken over as City Manager of Brigantine, at an annual salary of sixty thousand, plus benefits, which included a city vehicle. By the time he resigned in 1997, he was up to eighty-three thousand, plus.

Unencumbered by excessive feelings of loyalty, Chick was the type of political player who could maneuver just as eagerly for whichever team held the lead. Until obtaining employment with the city of Brigantine, Ciccarone had been a very politically active Democrat, involving himself with Democratic campaigns, both for pay and as a volunteer. Although he was not a Brigantine resident, Ciccarone felt compelled to re-register as unaffiliated once he went to work for the staunchly Republican municipality. Were it not for his fear of completely alienating all his long held Democratic contacts, Ciccarone would have probably just as soon declared himself a Republican, since his political change of heart allowed him to work as a volunteer for several Republican campaigns.

After conducting an exhaustive interview process, Ciccarone decided to appoint John Costello to the position of Director of Public Works. He represented to Costello that as long as John diligently and faithfully executed the duties required of the job, the duration of his employment in that position would be ongoing and indefinite. Costello and Ciccarone were both politically active in the community, and had developed a friendly rapport, which seemed to promise a sterling working relationship. However, it was not long before Ciccarone's propensity to constantly seek the politically expedient solution began to assert itself, resulting in friction between himself and John.

At first, it was just little things. For example, Costello sought to schedule regular staff meetings for after work hours, so the various department heads from around the island could maintain good communication and save a few steps on the road to getting things done efficiently. Ciccarone did not wish to attend these after work meetings. He preferred to go straight home after work, so the idea was rejected out of hand. Ciccarone also strenuously resisted the work order program Costello initiated. In private conversations, Chick explained that he was against the computerized system because it produced a document that was very clear on cost and accountability. John intended to run the DPW as a business, with an eye toward cost cutting and maximum efficiency. Ciccarone's reasoning, however, was more politically pragmatic. He continually complained that DPW had been budgeted a set amount of money, and that to fail to spend the entire amount was to risk a lower allocation the following year.

Appointed by City Council, Ciccarone knew all too well that he served at their pleasure. Therefore, he only thought in terms of how any given situation might affect his standing with Council. Rarely, if ever, was a decision made without careful consideration first being given to the political ramifications. When in doubt, Ciccarone's favored strategy was to do nothing and wait for a more concrete indication of the direction of the day's wind. Costello recalled that Chick had a stock response to any suggestion that involved the slightest possibility of invoking the wraith of Council. Ciccarone would always reply that his first concern was to avoid *"getting four or more of them mad at us. Then we're both out of a job."*

Ciccarone was not only worried about directly offending a Council member. He also steered clear of angering anyone who might potentially complain to or cause trouble with any Council member as well. This included DPW employees. One of the other reasons Ciccarone resisted the work order program was that it gave Costello solid evidence with which to make employees accountable for low productivity. Viewed in a comprehensive way, the work orders could be used to make comparisons between the performances of various employees on the same task. Once John began to hold the employees accountable for the patterns in their work habits, Ciccarone began to hear more complaints, which he hated even more than after work meetings.

This was not the only situation in which Ciccarone inexplicably sought to protect the DPW employees from perfectly legitimate corrective measures being taken, solely out of political concerns. For quite some time, John had wanted to install a video camera near the time clock, in an effort to curtail the problem of DPW workers punching each other in and out. Ciccarone would not allow it, expressing fear of some reaction by the employees.

Costello also disapproved of the fact that Ken Miller, whose very job title included the word driver, had somehow retained his job even after being convicted for DWI and losing his driver's license. John felt that such an employee should not return to work until regaining his driving privilege, if only to send the message that drunken driving would not be tolerated in a job where employees routinely operate heavy equipment. Ciccarone refused to impose any sanctions, instead allowing employees with no license to be picked up and chauffeured to and from their tasks, a perk unavailable to law-abiding employees. Another capricious decision fuelled by a Chick's constant desire to prove his authority.

Ciccarone had no time to worry about such trivialities as right and wrong. He only worried about keeping his job, and paid no attention to the complaints of the Wolfpack until they began to present a possible threat to his continued employment. Nose always in the air for a change in the wind, Chick knew that the Wolfpack members, while mostly imbecilic, did have a number of friends and family members in town. Most of those friends and family members were involved in various civic organizations, and might conceivably be able to exert negative consequences on Ciccarone with enough complaining to City Council. Even this remote possibility was too terrifying to countenance. Therefore, Chick was disinclined to provide any strong backing to Costello's complaints, preferring to play both ends against the middle.

As City Manager, Ciccarone had a duty to address the problems with some of the employees at DPW. Not only is it mandated by the Faulkner Act that a City Manager must see that all terms and conditions of the employee's contract be faithfully kept and performed, but as John's immediate supervisor, Ciccarone owed to it Costello to step in. John had reached the limit of his ability to discipline the Wolfpack, and their behavior had only grown more defiant. The city's supervisory network was set up as a system of memos and personnel files. By way of discipline, the worst John was permitted to do was place a memo in a problem employee's personnel file. Power to terminate or otherwise discipline an employee rested solely in the hands of Ciccarone, who exercised that power very selectively, and only when properly motivated. Like, for instance, in the case of Joe Wilkins.

When Costello took over the department, he and Ciccarone reviewed the staff in an effort to cut down the number of employees by clearing out some of the dead wood. Ciccarone took particular care to emphasize his recommendation that John lay off an employee named Joe Wilkins. That Chick would be so emphatic did not surprise John in the least, knowing as he did that young Joe was the son of then-Brigantine Chief of Police Guy Wilkins, one of Ciccarone's most hated enemies. The whole island was aware of the animosity between the City manager and the Police Chief, after the two had put on a display of drunken testosterone at the previous year's Christmas party at the Elk's Lodge, culminating in a physical altercation under the mistletoe.

Therefore, when Joe Wilkins, who had a history of sick leave abuse and who had once told Costello that he felt no obligation to do any work since his father was Chief of Police, went out on Worker's Compensation yet again, there was no problem getting Ciccarone's permission to investigate. The city hired a private investigator, who produced videotape of an obviously unhurt Wilkins frolicking and playing with his daughter, even throwing the child up in the air and catching her, at Storybook Land, a local amusement park. As a result, Wilkins was let go in what was termed a reduction in force. It is worth noting that Ciccarone never again authorized a similar investigation of any other DPW employees, even those with worse records than Wilkins had.

However, with the rare exception of the occasional strike at a mortal enemy, Ciccarone refused to wield his power. He assured Costello that he understood the Wolfpack's complaints were just a nuisance and he recognized that their objective was to disrupt operations at the DPW, but still provided no assistance in quelling their resistance. Because Ciccarone knew that the DPW workers and the union were simply retaliating against Costello's insistence on accountability, he repeatedly denied their grievances as lacking merit. However, whenever John sought to have transgressors punished, Chick disregarded the actual merits underlying a dispute and considered only whether disciplinary action might cost his favored council members some precious votes.

After a few months of constant conflict, the Wolfpack's strategy started to show results. Ciccarone had become annoyed with the ceaseless complaining and had begun to wilt under the pressure. Although Chick knew that all the complaints he was receiving were from people who had a stake in *not* doing the right thing, peace and quiet began to gain a higher priority in his mind than that of doing the right thing. Having been boldly informed by the Wolfpack that their campaign of harassment would not end until Costello had been replaced, Chick finally decided that it might be easier to join them than to go on trying to beat them. After thoroughly testing the wind, Ciccarone found that the initial groundswell of praise and support for Costello had calmed down as the public had gotten used to their newly clean island, and that the time may have arrived for his alliances to shift once again.

Although he privately continued to assure John that he placed no stock in the claims of the Wolfpack, Ciccarone nevertheless began to condone and support their behavior. He allowed the Wolfpack members to circumvent Costello's authority and instructed them to bring any complaints directly to him. This totally undermined John's position and destroyed his ability to lead, since the impression had been given that the Wolfpack was no longer accountable to Costello. John began to find that when they were assigned jobs they found undesirable, which was by now pretty much any job to which John assigned them, Wolfpack members would simply disregard his instructions and head on over to Ciccarone's office for some coddling and sympathy. This also served the additional purpose of destroying any morale that existed among the other DPW workers, who were not fortunate enough to have the City Manager's ear.

When confronted by Costello regarding this break in the chain of command, Chick's only excuse was to innocently claim that he could not stop the men from coming to see him. Nevertheless, most people involved in the city government at that time knew it was next to impossible to get in to see Ciccarone without a scheduled appointment. Not only was his office door wide open to the Wolfpack, Ciccarone even went a step further and furnished them with a drive-through window. Behind his desk, Chick had a window that looked out into the parking lot behind city hall. During hours when they were supposed to be performing DPW duties, Wolfpack members were frequently seen parked in a city truck alongside Chick's window, with the City Manager turned around in his desk chair, providing private drive-up service.

Ciccarone commonly met with these employees behind John's back, subverting the chain of command and encouraging them to become even more arrogant and out of control. Even if the City Manager never actually endorsed their plans, his tolerance of their actions most certainly encouraged their agenda by silent consent and suggested his support of their aims. As a result, the Wolfpack began to spend the best part of each day not working, but instead planning to subvert John's efforts to run the DPW in an efficient and organized manner, with the implied backing of the City Manager himself.

Interestingly enough, not even Ciccarone could deal with the bizarre Bobby Gibson. Although it was Gibson who complained about Costello most vehemently, he was the only member of the Wolfpack who was not invited to these private meetings with Ciccarone. His behavior was so out of control that the City Manager refused to connect himself to Gibson, dealing only with Miller, Hopkins and Lombardo.

When these employees would circumvent the chain of command and bring their grievances directly to Ciccarone, the City Manager would then deliberately withhold from Costello any information concerning the existence of the complaints, which denied John time to prepare any response or rebuttal to the charges. In an even more fundamental violation of his duties, Ciccarone also deliberately failed to require DPW employees to follow the established grievance procedures as spelled out in the union's Collective Bargaining Agreement. The proper process, as set forth by the Teamsters, not Costello, required that a written grievance be filed through the appropriate channels only after an attempt has been made to resolve a problem verbally. Instead, Chick met with the Wolfpack members in secret, gave John no opportunity to defend himself, and generated written complaints without informing Costello that a grievance had even been filed. By allowing this, Ciccarone encouraged the defiance of the Wolfpack and effectively stripped John of his ability to manage.

At the same time that he was ignoring the shenanigans of the Wolfpack, Ciccarone had also left John alone to fend for himself against the rapacious advances of councilman Frugoli. Despite frequent complaints from Costello about inappropriate or unlawful conduct by Frugoli, Chick made it clear he was not going to intervene, expressing fear of alienating members of City Council and losing his job.

The Faulkner Act clearly states that the City Manager has a duty to, *"Investigate at any time the affairs of any officer or department of the municipality."* Ciccarone knew that Frugoli should have been submitting all work requests through the City Manager's office, and that for a Council member to direct either Costello or a DPW employee in the field was a violation of the law. However, in this case the Councilman in question was one of the people responsible for appointing Ciccarone to his position, and besides, the two were friends. Of course, that fact raises the question of why, if the two were friends, did Frugoli resist submitting his requests to Ciccarone, who almost assuredly would have approved them, if not for friendship's sake then out of fear for his job? John suspected that the situation was either an attempt to entice Costello into participating in inappropriate conduct, or proof that Frugoli simply enjoyed demonstrating his power. Whatever the reasons, Ciccarone had a stake in keeping friendly Councilmen in office in order to ensure that he stayed employed. After all, should Frugoli be ousted or withdraw his support, a new City Manager might be appointed, a possibility that was to be prevented by any means necessary.

Although Frugoli seemingly had free reign to demand whatever work he deemed necessary for his ward, Ciccarone otherwise kept a close eye on which projects were completed and for which council member. Almost from the beginning, John found that the DPW was utilized as a political tool, and many of the decisions made by Ciccarone were based solely on politics and votes, and not on the best interest of the city or its residents. Chick often discussed his views with John, repeatedly stating that improvements to the city were to be done on a political basis. To further his agenda, he insisted on making all the final decisions on any improvements and major repairs to be performed around town.

To put it gently, the City Manager had his own re-election system in place. Another, more blunt way to put it would be to say that Ciccarone was attempting to pervert the election process. He took it upon himself to influence voting by making some candidates look bad and some look good. Members of Council who were on friendly terms with Chick received prompt attention when making a work request or reporting a resident's complaint. This quick service would be remembered at election time, usually resulting in an additional term in office for the lucky Councilman.

Conversely, Council members who were not friendly to the Ciccarone cause could expect no attention to be given to their needs. Resident complaints would be ignored, which would make that ward's Council representative appear to be ineffective. Such treatment was commonplace for Council members such as Democrat Ann Phillips, who inhabited a top spot on Ciccarone's list of political enemies. A common scenario would be for Phillips to repeatedly request that a legitimately necessary task be performed in her ward. After receiving assurances that the job would be taken care of, which she would pass on to the residents of her ward, the request would be disregarded. After sufficient time had passed to make clear that Phillips had "failed", her Republican opponent would be directed to make discreet inquiries to the residents regarding the problems they needed fixed. Of course, the Republican candidate would have no trouble getting the situation immediately addressed, which usually translated into lost votes for Ann Phillips come election time.

When John developed a comprehensive log of all needed repairs for the island, listed by order of priority and not political expediency, Ciccarone quickly confiscated the book and refused to allow it to be removed from his office. He plainly stated to John, *"I want that down at my office. I don't want certain people to see that."* Ciccarone was only concerned that unfriendly Council members not see the book and demand action in their ward. He specifically stated that he did not want Ann Phillips to see the book, reasoning, *"If she sees this, she'll want her streets paved, and I'm not going to do shit for her."* He meant it, too. John repeatedly requested permission to perform needed work in the third ward, regardless of the politics involved, but Ciccarone would refuse, saying that he did not want repairs done in *"her ward"*. Unfortunately for those taxpayers who resided in *"her ward"*, there was no tax break forthcoming to compensate them for this exemption from city services.

Throughout his employment with the DPW, Costello made a point of always documenting any event or conversation of possible importance, and kept Ciccarone informed of his every move and complaint via frequent memorandums. John also made notes of what response, if any, his memos brought. On many occasions, his memos prompted responses from the City Manager that were unfit for public consumption. Ciccarone, on the other hand, could not be bothered to concern himself with such trivialities, and rarely put anything in writing. Besides, things are much safer, and deniable, when kept on an informal verbal basis. So, while Costello had built a veritable mountain of documentation that could, in the wrong hands, bring about the downfall of the City Manager, Ciccarone found himself in what he considered to be a vulnerable position. At no point had Chick ever documented any criticism of Costello or his management style. No memos, letters or any other document were ever sent to John or inserted into his personnel file, nor do those files reflect that John was ever counseled in that regard. The City Manager found himself in a position to be going into battle unarmed against a heavily armed foe. Chick was far too savvy to allow himself to fall into that trap just yet. He continued to bide his time and wait for the right opportunity.

By the time the summer of 1998 rolled around, Costello had been complaining bitterly about the way Ciccarone used the DPW as a political tool, forcing the City Manager to wonder just how long it would be until his chicanery was exposed. John had obviously become completely exasperated with the combined antagonism and interference of the Wolfpack and Councilman Frugoli; Chick knew that his own refusal to offer any assistance whatsoever had ratcheted up the pressure even further. He knew as well of the reputation John had built as a political maverick, and recognized the DPW head as perfectly capable of going public and blowing the whistle on the whole sordid mess. Time was beginning to run out on this situation, the political animal in Ciccarone could sense it. And, as that animal is known to do, it was time to leave the ship before it sank.

Ciccarone began to carefully consider the political pros and cons of finding a way to remove Costello from the Director of Public Works position. On the pro side, getting rid of John would quiet down the employees, who by this time had become a real annoyance. Although Ciccarone knew that less than half dozen employees had actually made any complaints, he was sick and tired of hearing the Wolfpack and Costello complain about each other. Right and wrong ceased to matter once Chick became convinced that he would get no peace until John was gone. It simply became a matter of political expediency. Another pro would be the soothing of the fragile ego of Councilman Frugoli. Still seething over John's defiance of his demands, Frugoli also stood to suffer serious damage if Costello's allegations against him were to be made public. Besides trying to protect his friend, Ciccarone was also motivated by self-preservation, since he could scarcely afford to lose such a powerful ally.

As a con, there was to be considered the fact that Costello wielded considerable political power in Atlantic County. John still held the position of Municipal Chairman of the Republican Party, and was not an enemy to be made without careful consideration. Also on the con side, Ciccarone knew it to be true that John had done an amazing job in straightening out the DPW and getting the island cleaned up. Without ironclad justification, it was always possible that a sudden, unexplained termination might cause a public outcry and raise precisely the same questions Chick sought to suppress in the first place.

Adhering to his usual philosophy of inaction in the face of confusion, Ciccarone continued to weigh his options and waited for an opportunity to present itself. In the meantime, to make sure he had his bases covered in the eventuality that an opportunity to get rid of Costello arose, Chick began to develop an ace in the hole. He started an entirely separate relationship with John's Assistant Director of DPW, Ernie Purdy. The two held regular private lunch meetings without John's knowledge, where they discussed various subjects, including Costello, the DPW and Purdy's future. As Ciccarone's conflicts with John increased, his relationship with Ernie flourished even further, to the point where Purdy had seemingly almost developed into Chick's assistant, performing such tasks as installing irrigation systems on the City Manager's private property for free, helping Ciccarone move, and even walking his dogs for him.

However, even with Purdy waiting in the wings, Ciccarone was still faced with an uncomfortable situation. Costello was no amateur, and had so far been able to single-handedly fend off the efforts of multiple enemies seeking to undermine his position. Not only was John able to contend with a group of dysfunctional employees who spent the majority of their time actively resisting and subverting his programs, but he also managed to defy an unscrupulous politician with a god-father complex who thought himself above the law. So far, these two factions had been working independently against Costello, with little success. Ciccarone ardently wished to set up the convergence of John's enemies, since it was in the best interests of all three camps that Costello be removed as quickly as possible. However, the political operative in Chick recognized that despite the numbers arrayed against him, John still held the high ground, and to act against him without proper ammunition would be political suicide. Ciccarone would continue to silently encourage their efforts, but it would take an essentially risk-free plan to persuade him to abandon his passive role in the conspiracy and take active measures against Costello.

Then a city employee named Joe Manera dropped the perfect opportunity right in his lap.

9

Disfunction Turns Tragic

"He said he couldn't live without her."

—...Ruth Manera's brother, quoted in the A.C. Press

On the morning of July 22, 1999, tragedy struck in Egg Harbor Township, a sleepy suburb located approximately ten miles' drive from Brigantine. Despite a crystal clear summer sky, on that morning a shocking calamity darkened the day as two lives were ended by one senseless act of rage.

"I can't believe what I did here. I'm sorry. I just can't believe it. I don't know what to say. I'm just sorry."

—...Excerpt from transcript of audio tape made by Joe Manera

At approximately 9:30 AM, EHT Police responded to a 911 call from the home of Township resident and Brigantine Public Works employee Joseph Manera. Upon arriving at the home, they heard a muffled gunshot, accompanied by the sound of breaking glass. Entering the home, officers discovered the body of 41 year-old Ruth "Cookie" Manera, who had been killed by a gunshot to the back. Her husband, Joe Manera, 48, was found upstairs in the couple's bedroom, dead of a self-inflicted shotgun wound to the temple.

Further investigation revealed that a few hours earlier that morning, Manera had stood just a few feet behind his wife and, on the day before their wedding anniversary, fired a full load of buckshot into her back. Then he had turned the gun on himself and committed suicide. Friends and family were shocked, and desperately searched for an explanation for such a sudden explosion of violence in what had seemed to be a stable, if a bit stormy, relationship. However, as is so often the case in relationships, appearances can be deceiving.

"Sorry this happened. She was gonna leave me for another man. She told me the other night that ah, Fred Granese stepped into the picture and she was in love with him is what she was and she was gonna fucking leave me. She was gonna leave me. I could not take it. I'm just so sorry. I was madly in love with this woman. I was pushed to my limit. I was so madly in love with her, I just couldn't see her with another man. I just couldn't see that, you know."

Joe Manera had been employed at the Brigantine DPW for over twenty-nine years, and was considered by all to be a model employee, if a bit troubled at times. He was happy to work alongside his brother Nick, and had the respect of his co-workers, who acknowledged him as one of the most skilled heavy equipment operators in the department. But at the same time, Joe's personal life was a shambles. His wife Ruth was turning him into an emotional wreck no matter how he strove to conceal his problems; the strain was beginning to show.

Most of the longtime DPW employees were familiar with the Maneras and their on-again, off-again marriage. A hard partying couple that socialized primarily in the neighborhood taverns, Joe and Cookie, as Ruth was known to friends, were the kind of couple that seemed to thrive on fighting. Cookie was the emotional firebrand of the relationship, and had a checkered past of infidelity and brushes with the law, including an allegation of prostitution in Atlantic City from before their marriage. Joe, much more laid-back, but with an equally checkered past, could be depended upon to patiently weather Cookie's frequent outbursts and stay the course in their relationship. So, to outsiders, any recent evidence of discord just seemed like business as usual with Joe and Cookie. However, behind closed doors, the trouble was more serious than ever before.

Never the most stable relationship to begin with, the Manera's marriage began to deteriorate in earnest when Cookie received the news that she would no longer be able to bear children following a recent surgical procedure she had undergone. Although the couple had not yet gotten around to having children, Cookie had always wanted to be a mother, and she was devastated by the news that her opportunity had been lost forever. Her demeanor towards her husband began to change, and Joe soon suspected that Cookie was having another affair.

"Ah, she was no picnic either, believe me. She'd look for any excuse to put me down, trash me. I just couldn't take it. She wouldn't come home at night. She was lying to me, where she was. Then come to find out, she was with **** all day. Come to find

out the neighbors were telling me, when I would leave for work, he would be over here. I couldn't handle it"

Throughout their stormy relationship, Cookie and Joe had what might be referred to as sporadic fidelity issues, but had always managed to work things out and continue together. Joe suspected that Cookie might once again be committing adultery, and had his suspicions confirmed when an embarrassed neighbor informed him that a strange man had been spending time at his house after Joe had left to work. It did not take Joe long to identify Cookie's paramour as a former boyfriend with whom she had never completely broken ties. One can only speculate, but coming as it did on the heels of the sad news of a childless future, one might imagine Cookie's affair with a past lover to be an attempt to return to a happier point in her life, when endless possibilities lay before her.

Whatever the reason for her infidelity, Cookie made her intentions clear once it became apparent that her husband was aware of the affair. In past instances of unfaithfulness by Ruth, Joe had found that simply confronting his wife with his knowledge was sufficient to put a stop to the affair. However, such was not the case in this instance. This time, when confronted, Cookie defiantly admitted her extramarital relations and announced her intentions to leave their home and move in with her lover.

"I even asked her and she even said that her and **** had a special relationship and I ain't fucking stupid. You know how special relationship goes. I really can't take it, so **** can thank himself for this, he can really thank himself for this shit, you know. I just hope he has a nice life because he ruined mine and he fucking ruined hers. He fucking ruined it, and he fucking knows he did and he ain't gonna tell me no fucking different. Ah, I just hope you can let him, just let him hear this fucking tape and let him go on in life knowing that he did this terrible thing."

With his usual tactics suddenly rendered ineffective, Joe found himself set adrift. He had expected Cookie to repent when confronted, and instead she had left him. Joe desperately tried to get Cookie to sit down and talk things out, but to no avail. As a result of the stress of his suspicions, he'd been severely depressed for some time already, but the confirmation of all his worst fears had sent him into an even more dramatic downward spiral. The combination of losing his wife to another man and being left alone to wallow in his misery began to take a toll on Joe's health, both mental and physical.

"Mom, Dad...I, I can't believe what I did here. I just can't believe it, ah, I don't know what to say. I'm just sorry, just please keep on loving me. Ah, I just, I, I got sick is what I did. I got real sick and I tried telling her this that I was sick, really trying to tell her, Cookie I'm sick, I'm real sick. She just didn't give a fuck, she did not care, she just didn't care."

Manera's marital problems had been weighing so heavily on him lately that his work performance had already begun to suffer. His rate of absenteeism was rivaled only by the worst of the Wolfpack members, although with more legitimate reasons. Frequently late, absent, or with some reason to leave early, Joe developed a serious attendance problem. He was repeatedly counseled for missing time, but never divulged the true nature of his problems, preferring to keep his personal life private and instead simply claim sickness or injury. On the job, his demeanor, never the most outgoing to begin with, became even more gruff and brooding. As his problems at home reached their peak, changes were also occurring at work at the same time, and Joe had a hard time adjusting.

For most of his career, Manera had served primarily as an operator of heavy machinery. He had developed into a valuable employee in that capacity and been promoted to supervisor because of his performance. However, in becoming such a specialist, Joe had become used to *only* operating heavy machinery, which meant that during foul weather, or on a day in which no work was scheduled which required an operator, Manera could simply lounge around the shop all day and be paid to do nothing.

When John Costello took over as head of DPW, his reorganizing of the department included an effort to make the distribution of labor more equitable and efficient. John broke down the existing work into two categories: Fair weather work, which were tasks that required decent weather to be performed, and foul weather work, which were tasks reserved for times of inclement weather and could be performed inside the DPW facility, such as building maintenance and cleaning. During fair weather, Manera was almost always utilized as a heavy equipment operator. However, John could not justify simply paying an employee to do nothing, so during times when no heavy equipment was needed or the weather was bad, Manera was assigned standard foul weather tasks. However, Joe felt belittled by having to perform such tasks as painting a bathroom on a rainy day.

When Joe expressed dissatisfaction at this sudden change in his routine, the Wolfpack seized on this and ran to Manera with encouragement to join their cause and make complaints against Costello. In looking back, it seems obvious to John that the Wolfpack sensed that Joe was in a vulnerable mental state because of his marital problems and attempted to take advantage of him. However, Joe was not of their craven ilk, and instead approached John like a man and informed him that the Wolfpack members had been attempting to recruit him in their campaign to rid the DPW of Costello. Joe expressed his concerns regarding his work assignments, and John explained to him that he was not simply a heavy equipment operator, but a DPW employee with all the duties that entailed. Joe felt belittled by having to perform such tasks as painting a bathroom, which was well within the scope of his job. At the same time, however, Costello later promoted Manera to senior foreman and had also presented him with an award before City Council for commendable performance of his duties.

In 1998, Manera's performance began to decline noticeably. Usually an expert equipment operator, suddenly Joe seemed distracted and shaky. After a series of accidents, including one in which he knocked down an entire building instead of doing a partial demo of one wall as instructed, Costello took notice and sought a remedy. In an effort to refresh the skills of all the operators, John made plans to have the heavy equipment manufacturer come in and do a seminar on the operations and limitations of the machines. He ordered that Manera, along with several other employees, attend the seminar. Again, the Wolfpack smelled vulnerability and darted in to whisper in Manera's ear that Costello was out to get him. By this time, Joe was so wracked with paranoia regarding his personal life that he was an easy target for the manipulations of the Wolfpack. He began to buy into their depiction of Costello as a sadistic ogre, and allowed himself to be used for their purposes.

Under the guidance of the Wolfpack, Manera drafted a letter to City Manager Tom Ciccarone, claiming that by requiring Joe to attend the safety course, John was harassing him. He pointed to his long record of service, and claimed that John was over-reacting to an isolated incident.

However, by the time his letter reached the City Manager's office, Manera had already been involved in another accident. No longer merely resulting in damage to City owned equipment, this incident involved substantial damage to a private citizen's automobile. The accident occurred when Joe was driving a truck with a large rake on the back, which is used for grading the beaches. As Manera turned the corner to head into the DPW yard, the rake struck a private resident's auto that was headed in the opposite direction. This was no minor fender-bender; the rake ripped both passenger side doors open and broke the windows. Thankfully, no one was injured, but in light of such a serious accident in his department involving a resident's automobile, as well as Manera's recent past, Costello was required to investigate the incident and report his findings to the City Manager.

Upon interviewing both Manera and another DPW employee who witnessed the incident, John received conflicting stories. Manera claimed that a restraining shackle, responsible for holding the gate firmly in place when not in use, had broken loose and allowed the rake to swing out and strike the oncoming car. However, DPW employee Richard Brown, who had observed the accident from his own truck, told John that Manera had simply taken the turn entirely too wide and at too high a rate of speed, in seeming disregard of oncoming traffic. Inspection of the rake revealed no evidence of a broken or otherwise damaged shackle.

In a memo dated July 20, 1998, just two days before tragedy would intervene and render the issue irrelevant, Costello questioned Ernie Purdy on the subject of this incident. In that memo, John informed Purdy that he had received conflicting stories regarding Manera's accident, and requested that the matter be investigated further. Unfortunately, Joe was falling apart too rapidly for anyone to be able to help in time.

"I guess, ahm, I didn't pay her much attention. She strayed. Ah, I tried making things up to her and she just wouldn't go for it. I asked her to talk to me for, just for an hour, one hour. Just talk to me. Whether she stayed with me or she didn't stay with me. And ah, she kept trashing me, trashing me, trashing me. Ah, I just couldn't take it. I couldn't take it. I just hope my parents, her parents, her brothers and sisters understand this. Ah, there was just so much love there that I just couldn't take it, I really couldn't take it. Now that I did it, ah, it's too late now. I would have probably just let her go but she just got to it, ah, but she just got to that point this morning. Ah, she just didn't want to talk, didn't want to do anything."

Desperately searching for a way to convince his wife to come back, Manera hatched a plan to force her to talk to him. With the twisted logic born of obsession and desperation, he just knew that if he could only get Cookie to sit down and listen to him for a minute, he would be able to talk some sense into her. The trouble was that she refused to allow him to speak his peace. She was living with her new lover, and refused to see Joe or take his phone calls. Cookie waited until Joe went to work to come to their house and retrieve her belongings, and bit by bit, she was disappearing from his life. His only hope was to catch her off-guard and force her to let him have his say before it was too late. Then she would finally see reason and come back to him, Joe was sure of it.

On the fateful morning of July 22, Joe Manera left his house at the normal time, but he did not go to work that day. Instead, he drove his truck around the block and parked it on a different street, giving the appearance that he was gone for the day. Then he walked back to his house, went inside and waited in ambush for his wife. Ruth, under the assumption that Joe had gone to work, showed up at the house at around 8:30 AM to cart away another load of belongings. Instead of the empty house she expected, Ruth was surprised to find her husband, who, in a high state of agitation and toting a firearm, ordered her to sit down and listen to his pleas. Shotgun in hand, Joe once again attempted to convince Ruth that she should not leave him. When Ruth once again turned her back on him, Joe felt like he had no choice. All his rage and frustration burst forth in a heinous act of violence that would end two lives and change many others.

"I was…I was pushed to my limit. I was so madly in love with her, I just couldn't see her with another man. I just couldn't see that, you know."

As his wife attempted to walk out on him yet again, Joe Manera did the only thing he could think of to stop her. He shot her in the back from point-blank range. The blast from the 12-gauge shotgun nearly tore Cookie in half, but Manera was consumed by his rage and continued to fire wildly, shooting up the house. Strangely, no neighbors reported hearing any gunshots, especially considering the roar of such a large caliber weapon.

His frenzy beginning to subside, Joe's dawning comprehension of the gravity of his actions filled him with a despairing remorse. He gently covered Cookie's broken body with a sheet and made a few half-hearted attempts to straighten up his gunshot-riddled home. But his eyes kept straying back to the sight of his beloved wife lying under a bloody sheet in the corner, which was simply too much for Joe to bear. He closed his eyes to the carnage he had wrought and retreated upstairs to the sanctuary of what was once his and Ruth's bedroom. Wracked by grief and guilt, Manera maintained enough presence of mind to realize that he had been

scheduled to work on the beach that morning. Shifting his focus from his horrendous act of violence to more mundane everyday concerns was the only way Joe
could forget about what he had just done. Belying the wreckage of his life that
surrounded him, Manera made a calm phone call to the DPW office, leaving a
message on the answering machine stating that he had injured his back and
would be out for the day.

With that task out of the way, Joe's consciousness reeled back into focus and he
once again began to contemplate the situation in which he now found himself. A
plan began to take shape in his mind, but first, some damage control was
required. It was of the highest importance to Joe that his friends and family not
misunderstand what had happened. In such a scene of violence, it may have been
assumed by some that Manera had done what he did out of hate for his wife, a
possibility that he could not tolerate. It was imperative to Joe that he make clear
his reasons, not only so that everyone would know how much he had loved Ruth,
but also so that blame could be assigned to the proper party. In his grief, Manera
viewed himself not as a murderer, but as another victim who had been forced
into an unbearable position by outside forces. He wanted to make sure others saw
him that way as well.

No writer by any means, Joe found a more effective way to express his feelings to
those who might misunderstand. Tucked away in a bedroom drawer, he found
his old miniature tape recorder, the perfect tool for his purposes. Pressing the
Record button, Manera let forth with a rambling torrent of anguish and pain that
would allow no doubt regarding his reasons for what he had done and what he
was about to do. Finally, Joe had the opportunity to speak his peace that Ruth
would never allow him, and he attempted to make the most of it. In the end,
though, what the recording most effectively reflected was the pitiable state to
which Manera had descended.

His message to the world complete, Joe had reached the final scene of the tragic
drama he was acting out. He called 911 and summoned the police to his home,
informing the shocked dispatcher that he had killed his wife. Refusing to answer
any further questions, Manera gave his address and hung up the phone. Then he
reloaded his shotgun and waited for the inevitable conclusion toward which he
had been heading for some time.

As the police cars began to arrive at his home, Joe placed the barrel of the shotgun against his temple and, uttering one last apology, pulled the trigger.

"I'm real, real sorry that this ever happened. That's all I got to say."

10

Blood in the Water

When John Costello arrived at work on the morning of July 22, it seemed a day like any other. As part of his regular morning routine, John reviewed the messages on his answering machine from employees calling in sick. When he came to Manera's message, it did not seem to be anything too unusual, considering that Manera was frequently absent from work. However, as reports began to trickle in from various sources of a far more serious situation, it began to appear that something terrible had taken place.

Word of the tragedy first reached the DPW facility through the Water Department, when an employee received a call from his brother, a detective with the Atlantic City Police Department. As soon as the story came to Costello's attention, he immediately began to seek official confirmation on what was still just a horrible rumor. Captain James Barber, a longtime friend and head of the Atlantic County Major Crimes Squad, was able to affirm the veracity of the story and provide John with a few more details of the horrible action taken by a man with whom they had both socialized.

Upon receiving confirmation, Costello undertook the sad duty of passing the word along to the DPW employees, as well as the rest of the municipal offices. He immediately sent Ernie Purdy out into the field to round up the men from their various worksites and inform them of the tragic news. As that was happening, John passed the word up the ladder as well, contacting the City Manager, several Council members and the Mayor's office. He advised his superiors that he intended to shut down the DPW for the day, to allow the employees time to get over the shock and begin to grieve for their co-worker. By noon, everyone had been sent home. However, while most people were grieving, or at least wondering how something so terrible could have happened with seemingly no warning, others were plotting.

At the Teamster's Union hall, Business Agent David Tucker was in constant communication with the Wolfpack. Immediately following the tragedy, the Wolfpack and Tucker conspired amongst themselves to seize upon the tragic event as an exploitative vehicle by which to advance their agenda, in an effort to pressure Ciccarone or City Council to terminate Costello. Up to this point, Costello had certainly established himself as a strict boss and a stickler for the rules, earning himself the unending enmity of the Wolfpack and Teamster's Union. However, with the great job he had done in cleaning up the island, John had also earned the support of the residents of Brigantine, which made it more difficult to convince Ciccarone to act against him. Suddenly, there was now a way to get rid of Costello so that nobody would think to defend him, or would even want to hear his side of the story. Galvanized by the sudden opportunity thrust upon them, the Wolfpack set things in motion by seeking an immediate meeting with Ciccarone.

At City Hall, Councilman Frugoli had still not forgiven nor forgotten the defiance exhibited against him by the mere Director of Public Works. His insecurity demanded nothing less than complete obedience from his underlings, and he could not stomach the fact that Costello had so far successfully resisted his efforts to create the new road on the beach, not to mention his obstinance regarding Frugoli's illegal attempts to fix tickets. Even more distressing to the corpulent Councilman was the fact that, having solicited John's participation in his illegal and improper activities and having been rebuffed, Frugoli now found himself in the exceedingly vulnerable position of knowing that Costello could blow the whistle on him at any time. Fear of having his power, and therefore his very identity, ripped out from under him motivated Frugoli to redouble his efforts to convince Ciccarone to replace Costello.

In the City Manager's office, the wheels were already turning hot and heavy. For more than a year, Ciccarone had been waiting for an opportunity to get out from under the pressure of the anti-Costello factions both inside and outside the DPW. Not only had the constant harassment from the Wolfpack and the Teamsters Union begun to wear on him, but also Councilman Frugoli was not a patient man, and had begun to imply that perhaps a different City Manager might be able to rein Costello in a little better. Despite the ingrained urge to bow immediately to such pressure, the slick political operative in Ciccarone knew that making a move on Costello without perfect justification could be dangerous.

Besides the possible repercussions that could follow terminating John's employment without an unassailable reason, Costello also knew where all the political
bodies were buried in Brigantine and would be able to do significant damage on
his way out. Ciccarone had been patiently waiting for an easy way to get out from
all the pressure to terminate Costello, but still appear to the public that he was
doing the right thing. In addition, he needed a way to somehow ruin John's credibility, just in case he decided to blow the whistle and reveal what he knew about
some of the secret goings-on in Brigantine. Finally, the planets had aligned themselves perfectly and Chick's patience had been rewarded. The Manera tragedy was
the perfect opportunity for the Wolfpack, the Teamster's union, Councilman
Frugoli and City Manager Ciccarone to rid themselves of their common enemy
in one fell swoop, and they were not about to hesitate in making use of it. That
very day, a few scant hours after the shootings, while the rest of the DPW
employees were presumably grieving for their fallen co-worker, the Wolfpack was
locked away in the City Manager's office, petitioning Ciccarone for assistance
with their scheme.

That afternoon, once the furor had died down, Costello sat in Ciccarone's office,
commiserating with what he thought was his friend. Unaware of the underhanded machinations going on behind his back, John simply sought to express
his grief over the whole situation, but in doing so, unwittingly provided Ciccarone with an opportunity to set the plot into motion. After listening to Costello's
sincere expression of shock and dismay, Chick coldly advised John to prepare
himself for further heartache, as he claimed to have it on good authority that
John would be blamed as the cause of Manera's actions by *"the maniacs at Public
Works."* Shaken by this revelation, it never occurred to John at the time to inquire
as to how Ciccarone had come by this bit of information. It would later become
apparent that Chick only possessed this knowledge because he had been enlisted
to lead Costello straight into the ambush. One can only speculate as to whether it
was part of the plan to let John know that the accusations were coming, or if Ciccarone may have been temporarily gripped by feelings of remorse over what they
were about to do. Regardless of his reasons for divulging the plan, Ciccarone
quickly glossed over the subject, assuring Costello that no rational person would
believe such ludicrous allegations.

Perhaps to test his theory, the City Manager then provided the Wolfpack and
Teamster's union with a forum to make those very accusations by scheduling a
"counseling session" at City Hall the next morning. Ostensibly scheduled to pro-

vide the city employees with an opportunity to receive grief counseling or memo-rialize Joe Manera, it was actually a scheme to lure Costello into the same room with all his detractors and publicly attack him. To ensure that as wide an audi-ence as possible bear witness to John's humiliation, both Bobby Gibson and Joe Lombardo each separately contacted the same local television station and advised the news department to assign a reporter to attend the "counseling session." Both men spoke to Kara Silver, an on-air news reporter for TV40, a station covering Atlantic, Cape May and Cumberland counties, with a viewing audience of approximately half a million people. As any reporter would be, Silver was intrigued by the possible connection between politics and murder, and believed the DPW employees when they claimed that there was *"More to the story"* which would come to light at the next morning's ambush. Kara Silver took these "griev-ing" employees at their word and consulted TV40 News Director and anchor-woman Lisa Johnson, to discuss whether or not to cover the story. Eager to jump on such a juicy exclusive, Silver pressed hard, pointing to the fact that two sepa-rate DPW employees had called her with the same story of a man being harassed by his boss to the point of murder and suicide. On the strength of such seemingly damning testimony, the decision was made for Silver to attend the meeting, along with a camera operator.

With the media taken care of, the Wolfpack still had one more invitation to extend. In order to ensure that the Teamsters would be afforded the maximum opportunity to grandstand on television, Mike Hopkins contacted Teamsters Business Agent David Tucker and informed him of this new development, invit-ing Tucker to attend and make a statement on behalf of the union. When Cos-tello, who up to this point knew only that he had lost a friend and co-worker, arrived at the "counseling session", television cameras were already waiting out-side city hall. When John noticed a well-known Frugoli lapdog huddled in whis-pered conversation with the TV reporter, it did not take him long to deduce that this supposed opportunity to express his grief might have been turning out to be something else entirely. Although neither the camera crew nor Frugoli's crony was allowed to enter the closed-door meeting, the crafty Councilman still had another ace up his sleeve. Betraying foreknowledge of the ambush to come, Frugoli arranged for two police officers to be assigned to the meeting, in order to keep the peace in case of flaring tempers. One of the officers assigned to the duty just happened to be Frugoli's son James. The other spot was filled by no less than the Chief of Police himself, Guy Wilkins, whose status evidently commanded a ringside seat for the festivities.

Brigantine's city hall, which also houses the island's police and fire departments, was the site of the so-called "counseling session" which was turned into an ambush.

In attendance at the "counseling session" were approximately thirty DPW employees, including the Wolfpack and Costello. Also at the meeting, but attempting to keep a low profile were City Manager Ciccarone and Teamsters' business manager David Tucker. Two professional grief counselors had been invited to minister to the grieving, and evidently were not at all aware of the situation they had walked into. When the meeting almost immediately descended into a finger-pointing shouting match, the horrified grief counselors stood frozen with shock.

What had been veiled as a "counseling session" was actually a carefully planned ambush, a chance for the Wolfpack to make the big grandstand play for which they'd been waiting so long. Suddenly these four misfits who could barely summon the guts to mumble a syllable when directly confronted had grown into brave crusaders for justice once they had a suitable audience and television cameras waiting to broadcast their every utterance. As the meeting went on both Ken Miller and Bobby Gibson did their best to try to humiliate and defame Costello, while City Manager Ciccarone stood by silently. The "counseling session" was hijacked and used as a vehicle to disseminate the malicious propaganda of the Wolfpack, which was specifically designed to destroy John Costello's personal and professional reputation and drive him from office.

Miller flat-out accused Costello of direct responsibility for the killings, repeatedly yelling, *"John killed him! He did it! John put the gun to Joe's head!"* The ever-theatrical Gibson dramatically stated that John had caused the Manera murder-suicide, and then, pointing his finger across the room, intoned in his best TV-courtroom-drama voice, *"And now you're going to pay for it!"*

Costello tried in vain to defend himself against the slings and arrows being hurled from so many directions, but with no support from the City Manager, he was left alone and easily shouted down. All pretense of attempting to counsel grief was abandoned and most of the DPW employees sat in shocked silence as the meeting degenerated into a brawl. Entertained by all the drama, the police officers allowed the melee to continue until tempers threatened to erupt into possible violence, when they finally called a halt to the "counseling session" and shepherded everyone out of the private meeting and toward the waiting television cameras:

Later, Ernie Purdy characterized the "counseling session": *"It was kind of a crazy atmosphere. It wasn't a counseling session. I wouldn't perceive it to be a counseling session. I would perceive it to be a big brawl. It was just nuts, everybody was screaming at everybody. People got up and accused John. I think they said John killed him, John did it. John put the gun up to his head, something of that nature."*

Once everyone's grief had supposedly been assuaged, it was time to move on to part two of the day's well-orchestrated festivities: the media event. Anyone walking out the front door of city hall was immediately accosted by the irritatingly perky Kara Silver and her TV40 cameraman. Most of the DPW employees declined to be interviewed, probably still shaken up by the lynching they had just been forced to witness. Not so for the Wolfpack, however. In one of their few wise decisions, the more photogenic Joe Lombardo was elected to represent the Wolfpack on camera over the gawky and myopic Miller, the corpulent Hopkins, or the deranged Gibson. Appearing in DPW uniform, Lombardo stood on the lawn of Brigantine City Hall and gave an interview to Kara Silver in which he claimed that Costello had harassed Joe Manera and that John's behavior had, *"definitely contributed to it (the killings) heavily."*

Not to be outdone, Bobby Gibson found himself an audience and told lies that are even more ridiculous. Unable to resist the allure of the camera, Gibson added his unpleasant visage to the long list of things that should never have appeared on television. The wild-eyed Gibson ranted into the camera, claiming, *"Joe had talked to every council member, even to the Mayor, begging them to do something, please do something."* This was, of course, a complete fabrication, a fact that could have easily been verified by Silver, had she cared enough to check her facts prior to broadcast. Even a reporter for a high school newspaper could have checked Gibson's story with the council members themselves and found that not one could ever recall being approached by Joe Manera for any reason at all. However, as is usually the case in television journalism, not all the boring facts in the world can hold a candle to one sensational quote, and broadcast deadlines make everything a matter of priorities. It was more important to get the juicy sound bite than it was to confirm the veracity of the quote.

Our intrepid reporter also stated during the broadcast, *"**Many** of Manera's co-workers say they can't presume what would make one take a life, but they say that stress on the job was most likely a factor. **Most** of the workers believe years of alleged harassment by their boss, Public Works Director Costello, proved too much for Manera to handle."* Then the camera pulled back to show a group of dejected DPW employees walking away regretfully. In fact, Silver had only interviewed two DPW employees, not many or most, and the only two she did interview were the ones who had called her in the first place. Thus, the false impression was created for the television viewer that the whole DPW was of the same opinion as the two miscreants who had taken it upon themselves to represent them.

As the cameras waited outside, Teamsters' business agent David Tucker was ensconced in a closed-door meeting with City Manager Ciccarone. After making assurances to Ciccarone that he had no plans to make a televised statement, Tucker then proceeded to do just that, granting TV40 an interview on the steps of city hall in which he demanded Costello's resignation. Tucker says, *"The Union would request at this time that he would resign. The things that have transpired in the last few days demonstrate the type of stress that is put on individuals that work in this department."* Although this comment was clearly and unequivocally in reference to the Manera murder/suicide, Tucker would later ridiculously claim that he was referring to some *other* problem in the DPW. According to Tucker, the allegations made by the Wolfpack had absolutely nothing to do with his decision to make that statement at that particular time. He chalked up the many inconsistencies in his story to shoddy editing by the news crew.

The television broadcast went on to assert that Joe Manera had himself filed more than a dozen grievances against Costello. Yet again, even a modicum of fact checking would have revealed this to be absolutely untrue. Yet again, all these unsubstantiated claims were broadcast with no effort made to verify them. As a point of fact, Joe Manera had never filed any sort of grievance against Costello on his own. He had only allowed himself to be persuaded to add his name to those of the Wolfpack on one occasion, and that grievance was abandoned and never followed up by the Teamsters' Union. In the place of those facts, Silver instead alleged that the "dozen or so" harassment grievances filed by Manera were ignored because of Costello's political connections.

Despite actually being ordered by Ciccarone not to make a statement on camera, John felt himself being railroaded and, perhaps naively, sought to protect himself by granting an interview to Silver as he left city hall. Costello's segment aired as part of the same feature, but was so heavily edited that it no longer resembled the statement he had actually made. Gone were the parts where John stated that Manera had been a good employee, and that he and Manera had been friendly for years, riding motorcycles and going on vacations together. None of that helped feed the perception that the report was trying to create, so it had been left on the editing room floor. Also edited was the claim by Costello that disgruntled employees were exploiting this tragedy in an effort to discredit him and get him fired. Once again, it was all a matter of priorities. After spending all this time condemning Costello, to present an alternative explanation at this stage of the game would only confuse the viewers. Incredibly, while John was being interviewed, the maniacal Gibson actually positioned himself behind the cameraman and began capering about and making faces in a sick attempt at distraction. Costello pointed out the bizarre antics to Silver, who was forced to shoo Gibson away in order to be able to continue the interview.

Although City Manager Ciccarone claimed that he made no comment at all, nevertheless during the broadcast Silver said, *"The City Manager says Brigantine will address grievances from DPW more aggressively in the future."* Putting aside Ciccarone's denials, which the TV viewing audience never saw, a statement like this would seem to imply that the City Manager was of the opinion that the deaths did indeed come as a result of Costello's alleged harassment of Manera. It sounded like a promise to keep a closer eye on Costello in the future. However, even if the City Manager's denials are to be believed, other questions are then raised. For example, what should be inferred by Ciccarone's refusal to publicly comment and his order that Costello not give any interviews? The most obvious conclusion is that Ciccarone wanted the comments of the Wolfpack to be the only publicly broadcast explanation for the killings. Furthermore, according to city policy, only the Mayor, the City Manager or a Council member are permitted to give interviews regarding issues relating to the municipality. However, in this case none of those entities cared to make any public comment, so not only did the Wolfpack's claims go out over the airwaves unchallenged, they also were never censured in any way for violating the policy. Throughout the entire course of events, no city official ever issued any statement disassociating the city from the comments made by the Wolfpack members, which in itself would seem to infer consent and endorsement of the views aired.

The broadcast aired on both the 6 PM and 11 PM broadcasts of TV40 news on July 23, and at 8 AM and 6 PM on July 24. In a market covering almost all of southern New Jersey, with an estimated viewing audience of over 432,000 people, it is hard to imagine how many people actually saw the broadcast. Out of that number, one might wonder how many took the time to find out any more about the case than what they were told in the report. People as far away as Williamstown, NJ saw the broadcast, and suddenly John's home was flooded with telephone calls from worried friends and family. On the morning of July 24, things deteriorated, as the story was picked up and broadcast nationally by The Today Show, which airs at 8 AM and serves as a major source of news for folks preparing to head out for the day. By this time, the number of people who had seen the story, and had therefore formed their entire impression of events from the televised report, was inestimable.

As part of his whirlwind media tour on the 23rd, Bobby Gibson also found time in between television appearances and bouts of grieving to do an interview with the Atlantic City Press, the major print news outlet for all of southern New Jersey. Gibson again blamed Costello for the killings, and was quoted in the Press as saying, *"What happened yesterday was a preventable tragedy. If something would have been done previously, it never would have happened."* By way of evidence, Gibson offered up the fact that John had been in the midst of investigating an auto accident involving Manera's city vehicle at the time of the killings. It was the contention of Gibson and his band of merry idiots that Joe Manera was so upset over "grief" he had received from Costello for an accident at work that he had been driven to murder the woman he loved and then take his own life.

The accident in question was the incident in which Manera had seriously damaged a resident's vehicle with a large rake attached to the back of his DPW truck. Of course, since this incident had occurred just days before the murder-suicide, Gibson claimed that Manera had been *"out of his mind with worry"* over what Costello might *"do to him."* As was their wont, they interpreted a routine by-the-numbers investigation as a witch-hunt and implied that John had been placing "undue pressure" on Manera and seeking to get him fired. However, although the Wolfpack continuously sought to characterize the situation in the gravest possible terms, an uninvolved employee with no axe to grind described Manera's attitude toward the accident quite differently. *"He was a little bit upset about that. You know, like if you got into a car accident, how you'd react."*

Even City Manager Ciccarone stepped out of the shadows to give a quote to the newspaper, although he said nothing that could even be charitably interpreted as an attempt to diminish the perception that Costello was responsible for the deaths of two people. In the very same article in which Gibson shrieked his accusations, Ciccarone carefully sidestepped the issue and said, *"It doesn't serve any useful purpose to speculate why it happened. There are still two families to think about."*

Meanwhile, police and prosecutors were in the midst of a full investigation into the lives of the Maneras. Unable to find any evidence whatsoever of a connection between John Costello and the killings, officials quickly dismissed the theory being promoted by the media and focused on the details of Manera's personal life. Autopsies were performed the next day, helping investigators piece together the physical story of the crime. The tape-recorded suicide note, along with information uncovered during the investigation led prosecutors to conclude that the tragic events had stemmed entirely from domestic problems. Atlantic County Prosecutor Jeffrey Blitz said, *"The best evidence indicates it was due to a domestic matter."* However, as often happens in a case like this, the facts were completely ignored in favor of hysteria and innuendo. Before the story was broadcast on the 24th, the prosecutor's office had already closed the case. Nevertheless, the TV report was twice again broadcast in its entirety, with no changes made to the script whatsoever. Costello continued to be blamed, and no dissenting opinions were aired. Neither Kara Silver nor anyone else from TV40 ever so much as contacted the prosecutor's office for information regarding the Manera case, choosing instead to accept at face value the crackpot theories of a few disgruntled employees with an agenda.

Transcript of audiotape left by Joe Manera

Sorry this happened. Umm, she was gonna leave me, ah, I believe it was for another man. Fred Granese, ah, he sweet-talked her. I just loved her so much. I just couldn't take it. I really couldn't take it. I told her, I told her I would make things good. She just wouldn't listen. She kept downing me and downing me, saying a bunch of shit that wasn't right. Ah, she was no picnic, either, believe me. And, ah, she told me the other night that Fred Granese stepped into the picture, and she was in love with him is what she was and she was gonna fucking leave me. She was gonna leave me. I could not take it, I'm just so sorry. I was madly in love with this woman, madly in love and Fred can thank himself for this. He can thank himself for this shit. It would have never happened, but you let it happen. I guess, umm, I didn't pay her much attention and she strayed. I tried making things up to her and she just wouldn't go for it. I asked her to talk to me, just for an hour, one hour, just talk to me, whether she stayed with me or she didn't stay with me. She just kept trashing me, trashing me, and I couldn't take it. I was pushed to my limit. I was so madly in love with her. I just couldn't see her with another man. I just couldn't see that, you know. I just hope my parents, her parents, and her brothers and sisters understand this. There was just so much love there that I just couldn't take it. I really couldn't take it. No that I did it, ah, it's too late now. I probably would have just let her go but she just got to that point this morning. She just didn't care, didn't wanna talk, didn't wanna do anything. I worked hard all my life. I put thirty, almost thirty years in with the city. I was ready to retire and now everything is right down the tubes. I have nothing. Ah, I don't know, what can I say? I'm just tired. I'm tired. I'm real tired. We talked about going down to Florida when I retired within a couple years, and living down there, but it just seems the last couple months it just wasn't good enough. She'd look for any excuse to put me down and trash me. I just couldn't take it. She wouldn't come home at night. She was lying to me where she was, and come to find out she was with Fred all day. Come to find out the neighbors were telling me when I would leave for work he'd be over here. I couldn't handle it. I knew what he was doing. I know exactly what he was fucking doing. I'm not stupid. I wasn't born last night. He was boning her, that fucking...and I just couldn't take seeing him with her. I really can't take it, so Fred can thank himself. He can really thank himself for this shit, you know. I just hope he has a nice life because he ruined mine and he fucking ruined hers. He fucking ruined it and he fucking knows he did and he ain't gonna tell me no fucking different. I just wish you can let him hear this fucking tape and let him go on in life knowing that he did this terrible thing. He was the cause of it and he may say he's not but I even asked her. I even asked her and she even said that her and Fred had a special relationship and I ain't fucking stupid. You know how special relationship goes. I know for a fact, for a fact, that him and her had sex before. I know that for a fact. Ah, what can I tell you mom, dad? I can't believe what I did here. I just can't believe it. I don't know what to say, I'm just sorry. Just please keep on loving me. I just, I, I got sick is what I did. I got real sick and I tried telling her this that I was sick, really trying to tell her Cookie I'm sick, I'm real sick. She just didn't give a fuck. She did not care. She just didn't care. I'm real sorry. I'm real, real sorry that this ever happened. That's all I got to say.

Transcript of audiotape left by Joe Manera after killing his wife. Contrary to the claims of Costello's enemies, Manera's murder-suicide was completely motivated by his marital problems.

Lost in the frenzy of finger pointing, the Manera family had been left to grieve, forgotten. In the wake of such a devastating tragedy, family members can only struggle to understand how the loved ones with whom they shared their lives could have been pushed to such squalid extremes. Joe's family was understandably devastated and confused, unable to believe that the Joe they knew and loved could have done such a thing. It is not easy to accept that a member of one's family with whom a genetic bond is shared could behave in such an inhuman manner. Rather than face the sordid and embarrassing details of reality, many families in such cases find themselves pointing the finger of blame at some outside agent of doom, choosing to believe that their loved one could never had behaved in such a way if it weren't for *Him*. On the heels of the "counseling session" and the subsequent television broadcasts, it was not at all difficult for the Wolfpack to convince the Maneras that the real responsibility for poor Joe's actions lay with John Costello, who had harassed and abused poor Joe to the point of madness.

After all, Joe's brother Nick had worked at DPW as well; at least until the dreaded Costello had harassed him by arranging for Nick to be promoted to a higher position. The Wolfpack immediately set to work on Nick's head, and through him, planted their ideas in the consciousness of the Manera family. Once an easier, less painful explanation had been offered, the family grasped at it desperately. In another article in the Atlantic City Press, the family showed either utter denial or a complete unawareness of the truth about Joe and Ruth's relationship. Joe's family was quoted at length, describing a happy couple still madly in love, despite their rancorous separation. One of Ruth's relatives was quoted as saying that he did not believe that the couple would have gone through with their planned divorce. Of course, it is much easier to believe that some outside force caused your sister or daughter to be murdered, rather than accept the public revelation that she was unfaithful or had some other embarrassing private problem. While enraged at the casual exploitation of this tragedy by the Wolfpack, John knew better than to blame the family in a time of such sorrow and pain. They had simply listened to the wrong people, and while he certainly did not like being the scapegoat, John refused to misdirect any of his anger at the Wolfpack towards the Maneras.

Things grew a bit more complicated when the Manera family issued a decree banning anyone in a management position at DPW from attending the funeral. This was hurtful not only to Costello, but also to the rest of the supervisors, some of which had worked alongside Joe for fifteen or twenty years. John felt bad enough being forced to miss the funeral himself. It was even more terrible to have been the cause of others being denied the opportunity to pay their respects as well. Ernie Purdy, newly promoted to a management position, was not allowed to attend the funeral, despite his lifelong friendship with Joe. Purdy explained the family's motivation for such a strict adherence to their edict. *"Basically, in their eyes I was guilty by association."* The ban also played directly into the hands of the Wolfpack, who, in the absence of any supervisory presence that might offer contradictory insight on Joe's work situation, utilized their unrestricted access to continue to poison the mind of the Manera family against Costello.

During the week following the funeral, the Wolfpack continued to spread its propaganda at a frenetic pace. They made sure Brigantine's gossip lines were running hot and heavy with the story, and before long, the talk all over the island was that the head of Public Works was somehow responsible for the death of a city worker and his wife. Further details were unimportant, but were liberally added with each telling, just the same. In a touching show of dedication to the children of Brigantine, Wolfpack member Joe Lombardo's mother-in-law threatened to resign from the school board unless Costello was immediately terminated. To this day, the debate continues to rage hot and heavy regarding which was more laughable: Her overestimation of her importance in the scheme of things, or her willingness to hold the children and their education hostage over a political matter.

During this same period immediately following the funeral, the murder/suicide was also the subject of heavy discussion on local radio talk shows. Continuing their media blitz, the Wolfpack placed a barrage of calls to politically oriented talk radio programs such as the Don Williams Show on WOND 1400. Williams, who has followed and commented on Atlantic County politics longer than most residents have been alive, is a resident of Brigantine, and always kept a close eye on the little island that figured big in area politics. Since Costello took over the DPW, Williams had been one of his most vocal supporters, mentioning frequently on his show the much-improved state of the island and crediting John with having turned the department around. Therefore, when the accusations suddenly began to fly, Williams, who had a more than passing familiarity with Costello and his work, was shocked at such allegations and immediately detected the distinct odor of bovine excrement. Wolfpack members, along with their wives and girlfriends, made multiple calls, usually under assumed names, to Williams' show. Posing as *"concerned citizens,"* the callers would rant and rave about the horrendous treatment to which the men at DPW were subjected at the hands of John Costello. All of them stated emphatically that Costello was solely responsible for the Manera killings, and demanded, *"for the good of the community"* that John be removed from his position immediately. Williams, to his credit, was savvy enough to inquire as to how a resident who was not directly involved with the situation could be privy to so much inside information, which was usually enough to cause the caller to begin stammering and end the call.

In addition to these ham-handed attempts at media manipulation, the Teamsters' union began to participate in the festivities as well, sending out a mass mailing to any and all Teamsters' members in Brigantine. The letter, which was received by not only the city employees but also by FedEx delivery personnel and casino employees, was then widely disseminated throughout the community. In it, the Teamsters' union reiterated the accusations against Costello and again called for his removal from office. Interestingly enough, despite massive effort on John's part to obtain a copy of the letter, so great was the secrecy surrounding its contents that he was never able to get his hands on so much as a transcript. Even friends who had received a copy feared retaliation by the union too much to risk being discovered as the one who gave aid and comfort to the enemy.

Because of this barrage of propaganda, which had been primarily engineered by the Wolfpack, the erroneous public perception of Costello's responsibility for the killings grew and grew. John began to receive threatening telephone calls at all hours of the night from people accusing him of being a murderer, and noticed some friends distancing themselves from him. At work, there seemed to be an impression among the workers that it was only a matter of time until Costello was gone. Unbeknownst to John, City Manager Ciccarone had been making his presence known to DPW employees out in the field, asking questions concerning John and his work habits, and it did not take a meteorologist to feel the winds of change beginning to blow. With tension between Costello and the Wolfpack at an all-time high, Ciccarone took it upon himself to permit the troublemakers to start coming directly to him with their complaints about John. This of course not only served to undermine Costello's ability to manage, but also sent a message to the rest of the employees as to which side would probably emerge victorious in this battle of wills.

In yet another egregious violation of the Faulkner Act, Councilman Frugoli also began to conduct secret interviews in the field with select DPW employees. Of course, only those employees known to harbor animosity against Costello were interviewed, in an effort to slant the findings as negatively as could be arranged. Deputy Mayor Scoop Kay, upon hearing of Frugoli's activities, immediately advised the Councilman of the inappropriateness of his directly interacting with the DPW employees, to no avail. Frugoli claimed to be collecting information for Ciccarone, who evidently never knew he had the power to send city council members on errands. Obviously unsatisfied with his dueling positions as Councilman-slash-Godfather, Frugoli had taken on a third position as Ciccarone's very own private investigator. Just call him Councilman Corleone, Super Sleuth.

Of course, when asked, Ciccarone claimed to have been instructed to investigate Costello by City Council. Since Frugoli, himself a member of that very Council, claimed to have been instructed by Ciccarone to conduct his illegal interviews, one might wonder why the two could not get together beforehand and at least get their stories straight. One might expect that, despite whatever other limitations they may labor under, a pair of such crafty politicians should at least be capable of telling a decent lie between them. Then again, normal expectations had been shown by this time to have no place in this situation.

Moreover, just when things seemed to have reached the most bizarre possible level, John's world was turned upside down once again. Confident in his lack of responsibility for the killings, Costello had refused to allow rumor and innuendo to keep him from performing his regular duties. He had been attending work normally throughout the week of upheaval, and had actually begun to feel a slight lessening of the tension around the DPW shop. Things had just about returned to what passed for normal, which was confirmed when John entered the automotive shop to discover Mike Hopkins, who was no longer employed as a mechanic, repairing a trenching machine from Ken Miller's private irrigation business on city time. Ignored by Miller and Hopkins, Costello complained to Ciccarone, who had apparently already received a call regarding the same incident from Hopkins. The City Manager's not entirely rational response to the problem was to ban John from dealing directly with any non-supervisory DPW employees.

As illogical and arbitrary a decision as this may have been, Chick's order did serve to further lessen the ever-present tension between Costello and his small but vocal band of antagonists. Yet again, John was lulled into a false sense of security by Ciccarone's continued assurances that the whole situation just needed time to cool off. Instead of cooling off, however, the heat was being slowly and steadily turned up, until finally, on July 31, things came to a boil. That day, Costello received a phone call from the City Manager's office, requesting that John stop by for a chat on his way home from work. As requested, Costello drove down to city hall at the end of his workday, arriving at approximately 5:00 PM. Ciccarone, who for some reason expressed a desire to hold their conversation in the parking lot, met John outside the building, almost before he could exit his vehicle.

After a moment's small talk, Ciccarone got right down to business. As recalled by Costello, Chick led off by suddenly asking, *"What do you think?"* Still unaware as to the reasons for this meeting, John inquired back, *"About what?"* Ciccarone replied, *"About this whole Manera mess."* Somewhat surprised at this unexpected turn of conversation, Costello answered as honestly as he could. *"I think it's ungodly."*

With a deep breath, the diminutive Ciccarone squared his shoulders and peered up at the much larger Director of Public Works. *"Well, I want you to resign,"* he said with some trepidation. Totally unprepared for such an abrupt pronouncement, John's initial reaction was outrage. *"Are you blaming* **me** *for this?"* he demanded indignantly. He still couldn't believe his ears. *"No, no! I don't think it's your fault,"* Ciccarone backpedaled quickly. *"I just think it would be best if you resigned."*

John was unsure if Chick was giving him an order, making a suggestion, or just wishing upon a star. The City Manager was well known for his flights of fancy. *"Well, just how adamant are you that I resign?"* John asked.

All doubts as to the seriousness of the situation were removed when Ciccarone answered. *"Adamant enough that, if you don't, I'll terminate you."*

11

Et Tu, Brute?

John pondered his predicament as he drove home from his meeting with Cicca-rone, his mind still reeling. After the City Manager had stated his intention to either accept Costello's resignation or terminate him, the rest of the conversation was somewhat of a blur. John had managed to retain enough presence of mind to avoid a hasty answer and had instead asked Ciccarone for a week in which to think the situation over and possibly appeal to the Mayor or City Council to intervene. With what he'd figured would be the worst part behind him, Chick magnanimously agreed to the request, but added that the only way City Council could overrule his decision would be to fire Ciccarone before John's week had elapsed. The City Manager was accountable to the Mayor and City Council, but according to Costello's contract, the authority to hire or fire the director of DPW lay solely in the hands of Ciccarone.

Prior to the moment when he demanded John's resignation, Ciccarone had never once expressed the slightest dissatisfaction with his performance. Never once had a memorandum of any sort been added to Costello's personnel file, nor had John ever been reprimanded for any infraction or violation. Up until the moment of Ciccarone's ultimatum, John had been under the impression that he had been doing a good job, and while he felt very sad about the Manera tragedy, he had never even considered that it might cost him his position with the city. Neverthe-less, he found himself threatened with not only the loss of his position and income, but also stood to suffer very real, very serious damage to his reputation, both public and private.

John knew that for him to be publicly accused of responsibility for such a horri-ble occurrence, and then subsequently terminated by the city would create a strong impression in the community that the accusations were true. Unnerved by the dawning reality of his situation, Costello realized that he had woefully under-

122

estimated the ruthlessness of the Wolfpack. Although they had shown willingness to utilize any advantage presented by the DPW contract or union bylaws, John had felt secure in the knowledge that as long as he adhered to the working agreement, any claim against him would be proven groundless. His mistake was in assuming that the Wolfpack would stick to work-related issues in their quest to cost him his position and reputation. But even John was shocked and appalled that the Wolfpack would sink so low as to callously manipulate the feelings of a grieving family and utilize the death of one of their longtime co-workers to further their petty agenda.

During the one-week grace period granted by Ciccarone, John continued to attend work and perform his duties, while at the same time making an effort to garner support among City Council. He would find that the City Manager had already made his intentions clear to most of the Council members, with two notable exceptions. Deputy Mayor Ed "Scoop" Kay and Third Ward Councilman Sam Storino, two men who were well aware of the truth of the situation at DPW and who supported John's efforts, were purposely kept out of the loop and left out of any decisions regarding Costello's employment. Ciccarone announced his intention to demand Costello's resignation to the rest of the Council members as well as the Mayor, but still refused to give a reason, citing his right as City Manager to terminate the Director of DPW with or without cause. Although Ciccarone continued to claim privately to Costello that he did not hold John responsible for the Manera killings, he still insisted that John resign and still refused to state any reason, even in private.

Over the course of this week, John met with all the Council members and the Mayor at various times, conducting the meetings in small groups so as not to violate New Jersey's "Sunshine Act", which protects the voters from secret meetings of Council held away from public scrutiny. No more than three members of City Council may be present at any meeting that is not open to the public, so John was forced to meet informally with the Council members in groups of three or less. At all the meetings, Costello's theme was the same. He repeatedly informed the Council members that he was being ousted for rocking the boat and in retaliation for putting a stop to the corruption and abuses.

At the first meeting, with Mayor Phil Guenther and Ed Kay, conducted at Kay's home, John felt that he just might be getting somewhere. Both Kay and Guenther pledged their support and expressed the belief that John stood to be greatly damaged if he were to be removed from his position at such a critical juncture. The Mayor in particular expressed concern that forcing John out so soon after such a tragedy might send the wrong signal that he was being officially blamed. Ciccarone unsympathetically rebuffed those concerns by stating that since the accusations had become a matter of public record, it no longer mattered when Costello left DPW. Chick rationalized that even if he were to wait three months to demand John's resignation, some folks would still see a connection, so what was the use of waiting?

Known around the island as "Scoop", affable Deputy Mayor Ed Kay was John's most vocal supporter, repeatedly telling the other Council members in no uncertain terms that Costello was being railroaded and stating his desire to see that John stay on as Director. Nevertheless, even the Deputy Mayor could not get a direct answer from the City Manager. When Kay confronted Ciccarone and inquired as to the reason for Costello being forced from his position, Slick Chick arrogantly replied, *"It's my decision, I don't have to explain it."* Coming from the same man who regularly expressed to Costello his fear of losing his job as a result of displeasing too many Council members, it was a remarkably dramatic change in attitude.

All along, Deputy Mayor Kay expressed to anyone who would listen that it was his opinion that Costello was being forced out because of Ciccarone giving in to pressure applied by the Teamsters' union. Kay was quoted as stating, *"Almost since John Costello was hired, there was this clique of people who, I believe, in my opinion, had never really been asked to work, let alone to perform, and were never accountable for their day's work before. They were constantly in Ciccarone's ear about John, about being made to work, having to go out and do a day's work. And I think the Teamsters were putting pressure on John, and on Ciccarone. I guess you could say the Teamsters were harassing Ciccarone, by making complaint after complaint and it seemed that there was never any basis for any of it. Ciccarone never told me there was any basis for any of the complaints."*

The next night, John met with Sam Storino, Jim Frugoli and Richard Casamento at Storino's home. Third ward Councilman Storino, an Old-World Italian butcher shop owner and a respected longtime fixture of the community, expressed his full support for Costello and stated his wish that John remain as Director of DPW. A gentle peacemaker by nature, Storino pleaded with his colleagues on City Council to see reason and stand behind a man who had done so much to improve the condition of their community. Unfortunately, the presence of Councilman Frugoli proved so disruptive and hostile that all efforts towards calm reasoning were to be in vain. At one point, Costello and second ward Councilman Casamento were engaging in an encouragingly reasonable one-on-one discussion of the realities of the situation in DPW. Frugoli, taking notice that Casamento was actually beginning to listen to Costello's side of things, aggressively inserted himself into the conversation and intimidated the easily led Casamento back into towing the party line with which he had been programmed before the meeting. Cowed, the second ward Councilman refused to meet Costello's gaze for the remainder of the meeting and steadfastly remained by Frugoli's side from that point on.

For his part, Frugoli was at his filibustering best, remaining adamant that Costello resign or be forced out and expressing his willingness to bring to bear all the power and influence of his office to make sure of it. Frugoli announced that he had conducted a poll among the DPW employees, the results of which revealed that John was "*hated.*" He claimed that the complaints against Costello had been so numerous and vociferous that the only possible solution was for John to step down.

Councilman Storino, who had his own perspective on the complaints against Costello, characterized the situation a bit less dramatically. "*I see the Public Works guys a lot, you know, at lunch time and all. And what I do recall when John was superintendent was that John was a no-nonsense guy. He was a superintendent that wanted things done and they knew that they had to get their job done because John wouldn't tolerate anything else. So if that's in the form of a complaint…I don't know, I guess it could be a complaint, but I personally don't view it as a complaint. I view it as getting the job done. John's a good guy. He's a good man. Never once did I think that he would intentionally hurt someone.*"

Frugoli did his best to portray events in the most ominous possible light, making vague threats such as, "*This thing with the Maneras is going to be a big deal*" and "*If you don't go, things are going to get real ugly.*" His ability to predict the future aside, especially interesting is the certainty with which these threats seem to imply that John was and would continue to be blamed for the Manera killings. True to form, Frugoli's account of this meeting conveniently changed as time went on. As little as a year later, in an effort to cover his sizeable posterior, Frugoli described the situation as one, in which John had willingly left the DPW, "*because he thought it was time for him to move on and pursue other activities."* Even more ridiculously, Frugoli would also later claim that this meeting had taken place *before* Ciccarone's ultimatum to Costello that he resign or be terminated. In that case, what the purpose of the meeting could have been is unknown. Especially for Frugoli, who actually claimed with a straight face to have no idea why the meeting had been scheduled. Even when confronted with the fact that the rest of City Council remembered otherwise, Frugoli continued to insist that the Council members were not aware of the ultimatum at that time and had only met at Costello's behest. When pressed for any possible alternative reason for Costello to have requested such a meeting, Frugoli sputtered, *"I have no idea. He wanted to meet, we met."* Surely, we are not being asked to believe that the all-powerful Godfather of Outpost Four was at the disposal of a mere department head. Perhaps, to borrow a metaphor from the corpulent Councilman himself, the tail *does* wag the dog after all.

John's next meeting was with Mayor Phil Guenther, Councilperson At-Large Sue Schilling, and first ward Councilman Robert Solari. The meeting was held at the home of City Solicitor Tim Maguire, who also attended. While the mayor pledged his support for Costello, both Solari and Schilling expressed concern that unless John was removed from his position; they stood to lose votes in upcoming elections. Each cited examples of being approached by residents who had been woefully misinformed by the rumormongers, but who nonetheless threatened to withdraw their support unless some action was taken against Costello. No effort was made to correct the erroneous perception that existed in the community that John was in some way responsible for the deaths of two people. These council members simply noted the existence of the perception and applied it to their constant struggle for political self-preservation.

Sue Schilling, who could perhaps be most charitably characterized as inept but sincere, earnestly informed John that she had been told tales of what a tough and demanding boss he was, but refused to go into detail regarding what exactly she'd been told. She also refused to reveal her source. Schilling simply stated that she felt compelled to *"go along with this"* because of her deeply held religious beliefs and a resulting imperative that she *"do the morally right thing."* Conveniently enough, what she had convinced herself was the morally right thing also happened to be the politically expedient solution. In a later conversation with Deputy Mayor Kay, Schilling revealed that the person who had convinced her that the "morally right thing" was to oust Costello was none other than John's own boss, Tom Ciccarone.

Councilman Solari's excuse was that he had a longstanding personal relationship with the Manera family, and therefore could not possibly support someone who was perceived as responsible for their misery, even if he knew the perception to be a false one. From his perspective, whether John had done anything wrong or not was immaterial. The easiest way for things to return to the peaceful status quo was for John to resign from his position, so of course that is the course Solari favored. Costello also knew that Solari was another of Council Frugoli's thralls, and did not expect to hear much difference between the utterances of the puppet and those of the ventriloquist.

Mayor Guenther, one of the few city officials who recognized the realities of the situation, attempted to convince Ciccarone not to force Costello to resign. Guenther reasoned that for John to be fired or forced to resign at that particular point in time would imply that the city did indeed blame him for the Manera tragedy. Ciccarone, however, would have none of it. His coldhearted justification was to claim that, *"John resigning at any point in time subsequent to that event(the murder/ suicide), he was always going to be linked to it. If he had resigned three months later, the newspaper would have somehow worked into the story a link between his resigna- tion and the suicide."* By way of a compromise with the Mayor, Ciccarone prom- ised to issue a public statement to the effect that Costello's resignation was completely unrelated to the Manera murders and that John was in no way being held responsible for such a senseless tragedy. The City Manager assured Mayor Guenther that he would do everything in his power to avoid creating the wrong impression. Of course, once he had gotten what he wanted, Ciccarone promptly forgot his promise. He never made any public statement, even when solicited to do so by the media.

By the end of his week of meetings with City Council members, Costello saw the writing on the wall and knew he did not have enough support to make fighting to retain his job a viable option. He had also realized by this time that much more than just his job was being threatened. Unless he surrendered and stepped down from his position, John would be fired. In and of itself, while certainly not a pleasant occurrence, being fired from a job is probably not the worst thing in the world. However, when placed within the context of the situation in which John now found himself, being fired from *this* particular job, at *this* particular time was tantamount to being blamed for the deaths of two people. Considering the damage all parties knew Costello stood to suffer if this was allowed to happen, John was essentially being blackmailed to knuckle under or face a very public destruction of his reputation. Moreover, even by choosing to resign, John was not being spared much. The timing of the demands for his resignation, in the face of the public accusations by the Wolfpack, had the effect of lending credence to the accusations. Furthermore, the type of media attention Costello was receiving was pure poison to his politician friends, who had noticeably begun to keep their distance. Those like Deputy Mayor Kay and Councilman Sam Storino, who, because of sheer popularity, could afford to stand by John's side, were carefully kept out of the loop.

Still, as hopeless as the situation seemed, a part of John still wanted to stand and fight for his job. He honestly felt that he had done the island good, and desperately did not want to see the improvements he had managed to effect in DPW go by the wayside. Additionally, it was very difficult to admit defeat and give his enemies the satisfaction of seeing their cowardly conspiracy bear its rancid fruit. On the other hand, John was aware of the increasing effects of this debacle upon his personal life, and simply did not want his family's reputation dragged any further through the mud. As hard as it was for Costello to accept that his former friends and colleagues would stoop to such depths, he had no choice but to take their threats against his reputation seriously. Given the callous disregard with which City Manager Ciccarone and Councilman Frugoli had communicated their threats and intimidating demands to him, John concluded that he had no reasonable alternative but to agree under duress to resign, in an attempt to salvage what was left of his reputation.

Therefore, on August 7, 1999, John Costello submitted his written resignation, at which point he was asked to stop reporting to work. In order to compensate him for unused sick and vacation time, it was agreed that John would receive two months' pay. In a disgusting display of vindictive pettiness, Councilman Frugoli made a great show of insisting that Costello should not be allowed to receive unemployment benefits, since John did leave his position *voluntarily*, after all.

It was not long before Ciccarone had installed a much more willing accomplice as the new Director of Public Works. Costello's former assistant and close friend of Chick's, Ernie Purdy was elevated to the Director position. It would appear that all those hours of hard labor in Ciccarone's yard had finally paid off. Councilman

Frugoli was also on hand to help break in the new Director correctly. Within a month of taking over the DPW, Purdy had rolled over and built the Councilman his private road at Coquille Beach without so much as a whimper. In fact, the job was done so quietly that it never even generated any official paperwork. No plans were drawn up for the project, and City Engineer Doran was never notified. Neither did anyone bother to obtain authorization from the DEP regarding the encroachment onto protected wetlands. In fact, according to Costello, upon further investigation, no DEP permit could even be located for the existence of the entire Coquille Beach condominium development itself! True to his word, Frugoli also made sure that the dirty fill, consisting of asphalt, broken pipe and other remains of a broken sewer line, was used. The proposed improvement was never presented to the taxpayers, who were nevertheless expected to foot the bill for the Councilman to assure himself the block vote of at least one grateful condominium association. The project was such a secret, in fact, that the final job was never even inspected. When questioned about these annoying little details, Frugoli dismissed the matter with a very Godfather-like wave of his hand, *"It's a very small town, you know, we don't have to go into a whole dissertation. It's a matter of putting the dirt on the ground and leveling it off with a grader."* More importantly, it was a matter of securing a few hundred votes for the low, low price of some city-owned resources. Soon after, the city began to assert that the Coquille Beach path had existed since at least 1980, and that it was actually an emergency access road maintained by the city. These statements are patently false, as no alleged "emergency access road" is depicted in any official map of Brigantine. Nor is any such road authorized in any resolution or ordinance ever adopted by the city. Moreover, during his three and a half years as director of Public Works, Costello never once saw this road used by any emergency vehicle, nor did the city or DPW ever maintain it during that time. This road was actually nothing more than a footpath that was widened and raised as soon as Costello had been terminated and therefore removed as an obstacle.

Regardless of the environmental impact or legal ramifications, Councilman Frugoli was determined to have this road filled and raised along the
dunes behind the Coquille Beach condos.

While his former assistant was acclimating to his new office, John found that
despite his compromise with the City Manager, his reputation and community
standing had been irreparably damaged. Once his resignation was made public,
Costello was immediately replaced as Municipal Chair of County and Municipal
Chairman of the Republican Club without even being informed of this decision
or the reasoning behind it. When he inquired among those who would still take
his phone calls, John found that people simply did not want to be associated with
him because of all the negative publicity and media attention.

Also facing financial pressure because of the loss of his employment, John submitted numerous applications and resumes in the South Jersey area, seeking a
similar position, but received no response. He was eventually forced to return to
the construction industry for his living, but could initially only secure employment outside the South Jersey area. This caused additional stress, due to John's
concerns at leaving his family alone and vulnerable to harassment by some disgruntled person or group. On the occasions when John *could* get a job in the
South Jersey region, other workers who thought themselves familiar with the
facts inevitably mentioned his perceived involvement with the Manera killings. It

was common knowledge in the South Jersey electrical union that John Costello had been fired from the Brigantine DPW for harassing some employee until the poor guy went home and killed his wife and himself.

As a result, Costello had problems securing steady employment and was unable to maintain steady work throughout the following year. With every aspect of his personal and professional life severely affected, John began to slip into a state of depression. He found himself feeling somewhat embarrassed by the questions and accusations of the people in his life and started to withdraw into himself. Realizing that as time went on he was having a harder and harder time dealing with the stress of the whole situation, John sought professional help and consulted Dr. Edward Black, a respected psychiatrist practicing in nearby Ventnor. After a thorough examination and analysis, Dr. Black reached the conclusion that Costello was suffering from depression and prescribed a combination of medication and continued therapy in hopes of alleviating his patient's suffering.

With his personal life back on track and his mind much clearer, John was able to recognize that much of his stress resulted from his knowledge that he had been wronged. In the tumult following the Manera killings, events had been moving far too quickly for John to make many connections between them, but with time for further reflection on the situation as a whole, he began to realize that what had been done to him was not only morally wrong, but probably illegal.

While John may have been knocked down, he was not out of the fight just yet. He may have been forced to give up his position, but he did not intend to allow those responsible for his misery to walk away without answering for their actions. Galvanized into action by the prospect of dragging the truth, kicking and screaming, out into the light of day for all to see, Costello began to seek legal representation.

12

You CAN Fight City Hall

After extensive research and countless recommendations from well-meaning friends and relatives, John found himself in the Philadelphia offices of the high power law firm of Obermayer, Rebmann, Maxwell & Hippel. Founded in 1904, the Obermayer firm is one of the region's most respected law offices, with five additional branches in Pennsylvania, Delaware and New Jersey. Situated on three floors of the historic One Penn Center in center city Philadelphia, the main office is the hub of operations for the firm, and home to over ninety of the one hundred attorneys employed by Obermayer.

Designated as lead council was Gregory D. Saputelli, who served as the managing partner of the firm's office in Cherry Hill, NJ. As a specialist in complex civil litigation, the firm felt that Saputelli had the unique skills necessary to handle such a complicated matter. A former Special Assistant to the Governor, as well as a Deputy Attorney General, Saputelli had also studied extensively abroad, traveling to Russia as part of a governmental exchange program.

Greg Saputelli, lead council for John Costello.

On November 4, 1999, Saputelli filed suit in Federal Court on behalf of John Costello, naming multiple defendants, all of which later came to be recognized as three distinct groups. The city of Brigantine, City Manager Tom Ciccarone and City Councilman James Frugoli came to be known as the **City Defendants**. DPW workers Bobby Gibson, Ken Miller, Mike Hopkins and Joe Lombardo, along with Teamsters local 331, Union President and CEO JosephYeoman and Union Business Agent David Tucker were referred to collectively as the **Union Defendants**. Finally, designated the **Media Defendants**, were South Jersey Radio Inc, in the person of WMGM TV40, along with on-air reporter Kara Silver and TV news anchor Lisa Johnson. South Jersey Radio, Inc. is a South Jersey based corporation engaged in the business of operating several radio stations and a TV station, WMGM-TV, which is an NBC affiliate. Broadcasting on channel

40 throughout the South Jersey region, the station also reaches southeastern PA, as well as eastern Delaware and Maryland.

The first three charges alleged by the lawsuit were various forms of *Wrongful Discharge,* each of which each stood independent of one another.

The first count charged the City Defendants, (Ciccarone, Frugoli and the City itself) with violations of the CEPA act. CEPA stands for the Conscientious Employee Protection Act, and is also known as the Whistleblower's Law. It protects employees who blow the whistle on illegal or unsafe activities in the workplace from being retaliated against by their employer. Costello alleged that his reporting of the various ongoing abuses and illegal activities at the DPW facilities resulted in his forced resignation. This was potentially the most damaging charge, since employers found to have violated the CEPA act face much heavier sanctions than in a normal case of wrongful dismissal.

The second count of the lawsuit again charged the City Defendants with *Wrongful Discharge,* this time alleging that forcing Costello out of his job was a clear violation of established public policy, and that the defendants circumvented the law in conspiring to force John out of his job.

Charging that the defendants violated the law in wrongfully dismissing Costello is what is known as a tort remedy. A tort is defined as an injury, damage, or a wrongful act that is willfully done. This is different from what is known as a contract remedy, which led to the third charge of *Wrongful Discharge.* This count alleged that in forcing him to resign, the City Defendants had breached Costello's contract.

The fourth, fifth and sixth counts alleged *Defamation of Character,* and were filed against Joe Lombardo, Ken Miller and Bobby Gibson, respectively. This count charged that these three defendants had defamed Costello by appearing on television and purposefully attempting to damage John with their comments. In addition to the singular defendant in each of these counts, the city of Brigantine was included as an additional defendant in each charge, because of the city's failure to censure these employees. The clear implication was that the city condoned the defamatory comments.

The seventh count also alleged *Defamation of Character*, this time against Team-sters' Local 331, as well as against Union President and CEO Joseph Yeoman and Business Agent David Tucker. This charged that Yeoman, acting as the head of the union, instructed Tucker to make disparaging and defamatory comments on behalf of the union. It further charged that Tucker had participated in and con-doned the activities of the Wolfpack, lending the backing and power of the union to their disruptive and unlawful actions.

The eighth count charged *Defamation of Character* against South Jersey Radio Inc, in addition to Lisa Johnson and Kara Silver. This simply names the Media Defendants as those who willingly broadcast the defaming utterances.

An additional count of *Defamation of Character* was also charged against the city and "John Does two through six". This was an effort to account for additional defendants whose identities remained unknown at the time of filing. It stated that Costello knew there were others involved in defaming him, and that they might be identified as the case proceeded. This count prevented the complaint from having to be amended should further culprits be brought to light.

The tenth and eleventh count charged all defendants with Intentional Infliction of Emotional Distress against both John Costello and his wife, Barbara. For John's part, the reasons could not be more obvious. After all, this was not just a matter of a man losing his job. In their quest to justify their selfish desire to remove him from his position, his enemies had virtually destroyed his reputation and ruined his standing in the community. Barbara Costello's reasons for filing, while at first less obvious, were no less valid. This situation had not only affected her personal life and relationship with her husband, but had also interfered with her ability to maintain her employment with the city.

The twelfth count, filed against Ciccarone, Frugoli, all four Wolfpack members, Yeoman, Tucker and the Teamsters' local itself, alleged *Malicious Interference with Prospective Economic Advantage*. While certainly a mouthful, this charge means that these defendants had interfered with Costello's right to earn a living. Of all the defendants named in this charge, only City Manager Tom Ciccarone had any business whatsoever being involved in the employment status of John Costello. However, although it was within Ciccarone's scope of employment to hire and fire Costello, the lawsuit alleged that the City Manager had acted with malice in demanding John's resignation when he did. Therefore, the suit claimed,

Ciccarone had stepped outside the scope of his employment and opened himself to litigation as well.

Count number thirteen charged the Union Defendants (Wolfpack, Yeoman, Tucker & Teamsters' 331) with *Abuse of Process*. This charge stemmed from all the frivolous grievances filed against Costello by the Wolfpack members in their initial attempts to portray John as an unreasonably tough boss. In fact, *not one* grievance filed against Costello was ever resolved in favor of the filer. The union officials and the local itself were included because of their failure to stop this abuse, even after being advised to do so by the City Manager.

The fourteenth and final count charged the city of Brigantine and Tom Ciccarone with violating Civil Rights section 1983 against *First Amendment Retaliation*. This is a very serious charge, alleging that Costello's civil rights were violated when he was punished for exercising his First Amendment right to free speech when he pointed out the corruption and abuse in the DPW. The legal theory underlying First Amendment retaliation cases is that "a State cannot condition public employment on a basis that infringes the employee's constitutionally protected interest in freedom of speech."

Talk radio host and Brigantine resident Don Williams somehow managed to get his hands on a copy of the complaint soon after its filing. He devoted his whole show to the issue, reading the complaint in its entirety over the air. During the show, which was deluged with calls from outraged Brigantine residents, Williams contacted Costello in hope of eliciting a comment, but John was forced to refer all media inquiries to his attorney.

Immediately following the filing of this suit, there began in Brigantine a frantic scramble to obtain suitable covering for quite a few posteriors. The city of Brigantine, the City Manager, Councilman Frugoli, and, at least at first, the Wolfpack members were represented by the firm of DeCotiis, FitzPatrick, Gluck & Cole, based in Teaneck, NJ. Matthew Giacobbe, a partner in the firm, served as lead council, assisted by associate Peter Tucci. Specializing in labor law, Giacobbe met with city officials and attempted to formulate an appropriate strategy for such a complex and controversial case.

City Manager Ciccarone quickly made it very clear to the Wolfpack defendants that the city did not intend to provide their legal representation, since the Teamsters' contract required that the city pay into a legal defense fund for union members. The Wolfpack was dropped from the city's insurance and told to consult their union officials. While on the surface an economic issue, there was much unspoken relief amongst the City Defendants, who saw the inclusion of the Wolfpack on their legal team as a liability. Now they were the union's problem.

To represent the Wolfpack, as well as Yeoman, Tucker and the local itself, the Teamsters' legal defense fund retained attorney Peter Marks Sr., a solo practitioner from Northfield, NJ. Marks' legal strategy consisted of little more than making copies of any documents filed by the city's attorneys, in order to file them again on behalf of his clients.

South Jersey Radio, the owner of TV40 and the employer of Lisa Johnson and Kara Silver, retained the Atlantic City firm of Fox, Rothschild, O'Brien & Frankel. Firm partner Jack Gorny appeared for the defense, accompanied by associate Sherri Affrunti. It was only after everyone had finally secured representation that the defendants were divided, for purposes of clarity, into the three designations of Media, City and Union Defendants.

Once it had become clear just who would be representing whom, the legal wrangling began. John found himself seated at ringside for the greatest show on earth. So far, John had been receiving quite an education in the world of litigation, but Greg Saputelli assured him that he had seen nothing yet. Every person even obliquely involved with the case had been subpoenaed, and judging by some of the personalities involved, the depositions were going to be very interesting.

13

Speak No Evil

Just how serious a potential threat to the status quo this case represented became clear once John Costello had been deposed. In his testimony, Costello went into detail regarding the litany of abuses in the DPW. Of course, to the higher-level city officials, John's revelations came as no surprise, since they had forced him out of his job to protect the very secrets he was now revealing. However, to many of the rank-and-file workers, most of whom with no more experience in civil litigation than an appearance or two on the wrong end of landlord-tenant court, Costello's deposition was cause for great concern.

The members of the Wolfpack, operating with an agenda of paranoia even in the best of times, had been driven even further over the edge by the city's decision to refuse them representation. Despite the assurances of the City Manager to the contrary, the Wolfpack began to suspect that they were being positioned to serve as a sacrifice, should one become necessary to spare the city embarrassment or expense. Once the allegations in Costello's deposition were made public, however, their paranoia reached a truly frenzied pitch, and they decided it was time to go back on the offensive.

In June of 2000, Wolfpack member Mike Hopkins somehow obtained a copy of Costello's deposition and brought the document into the DPW facility. Choosing only the most inflammatory excerpts, Hopkins gleefully read aloud from the deposition, with the obvious intention of inciting ill will towards Costello among the DPW employees, particularly any who might previously have testified on John's behalf. As the subsequent depositions were conducted, it became apparent that the Wolfpack's design had had the desired effect on at least some of the DPW employees. The main target of Hopkins' strategy was Water Department supervisor Carmen Danunzio, who was perceived as an ally of Costello. Most of the segments of testimony quoted were in reference to Danunzio, who turned out to be an easy target for the Wolfpack's manipulation.

A year or so prior, DPW receptionist Kelly Wilson had verbally complained to Costello that the 65 year-old Danunzio had been making her uncomfortable at work by frequently touching her and making sexual statements and "dirty jokes" in her presence. John immediately met with Danunzio, advised him of Wilson's allegations, and counseled him that such behavior could not continue. The matter was settled without further incident and had been relegated to the past until Costello was asked about the situation during the course of his deposition. With sadistic delight, Hopkins read the passages regarding this incident in front of an entire room full of DPW employees, which understandably embarrassed and angered Danunzio, who reacted in just the manner the Wolfpack had hoped he would. His first act was to protest too much by confronting Kelly Wilson and demanding that she type up and sign a letter confirming that Danunzio had never sexually harassed her. Of course, the letter made no mention of whether Wilson denied making the initial complaint to Costello regarding Carmen's harassment, but at least it made him feel better. For whatever reason, Danunzio then had the letter notarized.

Apparently satisfied that he had proven his innocence, Danunzio next set himself at the task of gaining vengeance for his perceived humiliation at the hands of John Costello, who, it should be noted, was not the one who purposefully embarrassed Carmen in front of his co-workers. Nevertheless, Danunzio's pride demanded that he avenge himself during his own deposition, and he embarked on a crusade to embarrass and smear Costello in the same way he felt that he had been. Five minutes before he was scheduled to testify, once witnesses who could refute his story had already been deposed, Danunzio produced a surprise document accusing Costello of a litany of inappropriate and unprofessional statements, including horrifying comments regarding the Manera killings. After preparing this list, Carmen had then gathered a group of his subordinates who were then ordered to sign it, attesting that they had all heard Costello make these statements as well.

Among the most ridiculous accusations made by Danunzio on this document was his claim that, on the day of the Manera killings, in front of himself and a room full of employees, Costello had replied, *"One down, one to go"* when informed of Joe Manera's death. While of course Costello denies the comment, an obvious and repugnant reference to Joe's brother Nick, it is perhaps more telling that no other defendant in the case was willing to corroborate this story, or even believe that it had actually occurred. Such was the absurdity of this accusation that an even greater shadow of doubt was cast on the already questionable credibility of Danunzio's entire testimony. The production of the list at the last possible minute was obviously a calculated attempt to deny John's attorneys the opportunity to obtain discovery that would further impeach the credibility of this "document". When Costello's attorneys then sought to take further testimony of two of the alleged witnesses to these statements, both of whom had already testified, the city's lawyers objected and argued that it was too late to schedule any more depositions.

Danunzio's list also made pathetic claims of racist statements by Costello that did not stand up under questioning, and revealed just whom the real racist was. When John's attorney, Greg Saputelli, challenged him to back up these assertions, Danunzio justified his reasoning by stating, *"He didn't like niggers."* Saputelli then asked what exactly Costello had said that would lead Carmen to such a conclusion, to which Danunzio replied, *"He said 'I don't like niggers.'"* Astonished by the witness' seeming obliviousness to the absurdity of this exchange, which seemed more suitable for an episode of *Seinfeld* than a civil deposition, Saputelli asked, *"In those words?"* Carmen's deadpan reply was *"Yeah."* In an exchange that would be amusing if not for the pathetically obvious racism, Saputelli continued this line of questioning. *"Other than this statement, what else did he say specifically, if you recall?"* Danunzio replied, *"About niggers? Is that what you mean?"* Saputelli winced at the casual slur. *"About black people. But you call them what you want."* he replied. Danunzio, completely insensitive to the crudity of his remarks, simply shrugged and replied, *"Okay."*

As for the provenance of the list, Danunzio claimed that he had compiled the document from notes he had made contemporaneously at the times Costello had made the comments. He would have liked to produce the original notes, which he claimed were even dated, but unfortunately, they had been accidentally "thrown away". Even more unfortunately, at least for him, that story does not check out, either, because Carmen Danunzio was, and for that matter might still be, functionally illiterate. With no formal education beyond eighth grade and virtually nonexistent reading and writing skills, Carmen had to have important documents read to him by subordinates. An otherwise undistinguished DPW employee was promoted to Senior Foreman so he could serve as Danunzio's unofficial assistant. This employee did all Danunzio's reading and writing for him. In fact, the list of comments supposedly made by Costello, which was supposedly transcribed from an illiterate man's handwritten notes, was actually in the handwriting of Danunzio's assistant. Presumably, unlike Kelly Wilson, one employee did not mind taking a little of Carmen's dictation.

It is enough to make one's heart swell with pride at the opportunities available in this great land of ours, even for those poor unfortunates who never learned to read or write. Nevertheless, one question still demands to be asked. How does an illiterate man rise to the position of Supervisor of the Water Department? Danunzio started work with the DPW in 1973, and was promoted first to Foreman and then Senior Foreman by then-Superintendent Robert Gibson Sr. Both times, one would have to presume that he was promoted over men who could read. So what was it about Carmen that so distinguished him from the rest of the pack that Gibson picked him despite his illiteracy? Was it because he had a natural genius for the pumping and distribution of water? Alternatively, could there have been some other, less obvious reason?

A possible explanation arose when, a few years into his tenure as Supervisor, Danunzio was investigated, along with Gibson Sr., for receiving kickbacks from chemical sales representatives. Allegedly, Gibson and Danunzio had entered into a clandestine agreement with chemical salesmen to dilute water-treatment chemicals that the city purchased. For example, suppose the city needed ten gallons of a certain chemical. The salesman would deliver five gallons, to which Gibson and Carmen would allegedly add five gallons of water. The city would still be charged for ten gallons, and the two budding entrepreneurs from the Water Dept. would split the profits with the salesman. On a scale of thousands of gallons of chemicals per year, the scheme must have been lucrative enough to justify supplying inadequate water treatment to the island's residents, including their own families.

During his deposition, Danunzio also went out of his way to portray himself as a defender of poor Joe Manera. Carmen claimed to have complained to the City Manager about skilled workers being assigned to busy work, after John assigned Manera to paint a bathroom. On the other hand, this staunch defender of Joe Manera had been the one to report to Costello that Manera would deliberately disable "his" machine before he went on vacation, so that nobody else could do his heavy equipment work while he was away. City Manager Ciccarone did not recall Carmen ever complaining to him about Costello, but did admit during his own deposition that at various times he had considered demoting Danunzio, because he was *"not satisfied with his performance as a supervisor."*

Danunzio repeatedly shot himself in the foot throughout his deposition, managing to let it slip out that he had a girlfriend outside his marriage, used drugs, operated his candle-making business on city time, and frequently carried an illegal handgun. At age 65, with two jobs, a wife and a girlfriend, it was no wonder he had never found time to learn to read. Not only did he make candles, but he burned them at both ends as well. By the time his deposition ended, Danunzio had embarrassed himself more than anyone else and shown himself to be nothing more than a man with an axe to grind.

However, the entertainment was far from over. The rest of the depositions, while slightly less dramatic, proved no less interesting. First to be deposed after Costello were the members of the Wolfpack. Interestingly, neither side sought to elicit testimony from the volatile Bobby Gibson. While it was certainly no surprise that John's attorneys avoided giving Gibson a platform from which to spew his venom, it came as a shock to most observers that such a seemingly tailor-made weapon for the defense would be left unused. Evidently, even the master sculptor must beware, lest the knife he uses turn against his own hand. Since not even the defense attorneys wanted anything to do with him, Gibson found himself excluded from the proceedings almost entirely, which was perhaps an even worse punishment than any court could impose.

The remaining Wolfpack members were deposed, and their testimony ranged from tight-lipped reticence all the way to arrogant braggadocio, sometimes all within the same answer. Mike Hopkins, the corpulent union shop steward, stuck mostly with the former course, and as a result, did himself the least damage. At first, Hopkins denied reading comments regarding Carmen Danunzio from Costello's deposition aloud to a roomful of DPW employees. Nevertheless, when cornered, he was forced to admit that he had read *something* aloud; he just did not know what a deposition *was*. As union shop steward, Hopkins had a duty to possess an enhanced understanding of the collective bargaining agreement between the city and the Teamsters, with regard to the DPW. However, under questioning, Hopkins displayed very little familiarity with the terms of the contract he had been appointed to uphold on the job, admitting at one point, *"I don't have it memorized. I've seen it."* Despite his ignorance, Hopkins had been invited to attend contract negotiations between the city and the Teamsters' local, at which he held up the proceedings by failing to bring with him the contract proposal, which had been presented to him for submittal to the union. When asked why he had not brought the document, Hopkins had replied, *"I wiped my ass with it"*, much to the embarrassment of the Teamsters' negotiator brought in for what he must have thought would be a professionally conducted meeting. When questioned about this episode, Hopkins proudly admitted to the unseemly remarks, perhaps irrationally regarding himself as a tough negotiator in his own right. It should be noted that Hopkins was not invited to subsequent negotiations.

As the depositions proceeded, a new approach to the story began to emerge. Contrary to previous the party line, which held that Costello was not held at all responsible for the Manera killings, but was instead forced out due to his management style, the Wolfpack simply could not resist carrying their campaign of slander into the legal arena. In the depositions of both Ken Miller and Joe Lombardo, both defendants made several allegations claiming that Costello had in fact harassed Joe Manera to the brink of murder and suicide. To support this charge, Miller suddenly claimed to have had some sort of special relationship with Manera, one in which both men had really opened up about their personal problems to one another and, as a result, had become very close. However, in the course of revealing personal problems and becoming so close, Manera never once confided to Miller that he had been having problems with his marriage, even when he and his wife had separated. Miller testified that he had comforted his very close friend, who was terrified that Costello would use his political influence to have Manera fired. He also admitted that the responsibility for planting that very idea in Manera's head lay with him and his Wolfpack cronies. Miller himself stated that they had been in Joe's ear about Costello as little as three days before the killings.

Possessed of an arrogant but ultimately dull-witted bravery, Miller freely admitted to many of the allegations made in John Costello's deposition, even to offenses to which the rest of his compatriots had been intelligent enough to respond with denials. Miller made no bones about affirming that he and several other employees had routinely punched each other's time cards, or that he had a habit of taking off Mondays and Fridays with pay. However, when discussing the incident in which Costello had checked with the Galloway Township Sewer Department after Miller took a paid day off due to an "emergency sewer problem", he grew visibly angry. Surprisingly, his wrath was not due to a perceived invasion of his privacy, as one might presume. Instead, Miller said, *"I was infuri-*

ated. He wasted MY tax dollars to send someone to my house. That's not Brigantine. That's MY tax dollars." Like most of us, apparently, Ken Miller would rather live in a town where the tax dollars spent on Public Works employees are *not* a waste of money.

Joe Lombardo also jumped on the bandwagon and declared that he too had developed a special relationship with Joe Manera. Echoing Miller, he testified that Manera had been *"a wreck"* with worry regarding Costello's reaction to a recent accident in a city truck, but Lombardo took things a step further, going so far as to express annoyance with his good friend. *"It was almost irritating because that's all I ever heard out of his mouth for about a year to a year and a half. He was obsessed."* No other DPW employees, even the ones with whom he had apparently just begun special relationships, could corroborate Manera's supposed obsession. In addition, despite their "close friendship," Lombardo was also unaware of Manera's marital problems. Apparently, Manera had been so obsessed with thoughts of John Costello that he had no time to discuss his crumbling marriage and financial problems with his good friends. Implying some dark secret, Lombardo intoned ominously, *"Joe confided in me what was going on between him and Costello."* When asked under oath to recount the details of such conversations, Lombardo stubbornly refused to answer, citing some sort of absurd privilege that protected him from having to repeat what Manera had said to him "in confidence."

Of the three Wolfpack members deposed, Lombardo definitely proved to be the most truculent, disputing every petty little detail and only grudgingly parceling out the truth when cornered. In his quest to cast Costello in as bad a light as possible, Lombardo claimed that John only issued memos to deliver criticism and condemnation, and never for any positive reason. However, when confronted with a positive memo, one in fact praising *him*, Lombardo actually suggested that it must have been the only one John had ever sent.

For some reason, Lombardo also stubbornly denied having contacted TV40 regarding the "counseling session" at city hall. Predictably, his denials were immediately refuted by the testimony of TV40's on-air reporter, Kara Silver, who confirmed that she had received a phone call from Joe Lombardo informing her of the "counseling session" and suggesting that she attend.

In the course of being deposed, Kara Silver candidly confessed that she had made a mistake in taking the word of some admittedly dubious sources without doing any investigation on her own to verify the details of the story. She also expressed regret in having allowed herself to be used by the Wolfpack. However, not all of the misstatements in the broadcast could be attributed to Silver being misled. As part of her voice-over narration of the story, Silver had gravely intoned, "*The Prosecutor says Manera shot his wife to death and then turned the gun on himself.*" This would seem to infer that she had communicated with the Prosecutor's office and had obtained the information for her story, including the allegations of job stress as a cause, from this impeccable source. Instead, Silver admitted under questioning that she had never contacted the Prosecutor's office, although she knew that she should have. Had she bothered to exert this minimal journalistic effort, the story might not have aired at all, since Silver would have been informed that the case had already been closed as resulting from a domestic matter.

Concerning Costello's complaints about the questionable editing of his interview, she said, "*There are plenty of times when a reporter goes to interview someone, the person will think that everything they're saying is going to be on the air. We have a time limit, so there are many times when things are cut out.*" Such a seemingly reasonable explanation does very little, however, to justify the way the entire piece was slanted against Costello. Kara Silver had written and edited the segment herself, and made a conscious decision regarding what story she wanted to tell.

Silver laid responsibility for the rest of the misinformation contained in the broadcast at the feet of Teamsters' business agent David Tucker. In fact, Silver insisted that Tucker provided most of the incorrect information contained in the report to her. She claimed that it had been Tucker who had told her that there had been "dozens of grievances" filed against Costello, and that John's powerful political connections had enabled him to have the complaints squashed.

Of course, David Tucker emphatically denied making any of these statements, a claim made slightly more believable upon examination of his deposition, wherein he specializes in saying nothing at all. Especially uncooperative, even among a group of defendants not exactly disposed to giving helpful answers to the plaintiff, Tucker led the field in "*I don't recall*" responses, with strings of six to ten questions at a time being evaded in this manner. Seeking to short-circuit speculation that the Teamsters' local was motivated to oust Costello because of his intention to privatize certain aspects of the DPW, Tucker was quick to deny that he had even been aware of such intentions on John's part. Unfortunately, this assertion was contradicted by the testimony of the three Wolfpack members, who claimed to have frequently discussed that very subject with union officials, including Tucker.

Throughout the deposition process, several other DPW employees were deposed by Costello's attorneys in an attempt to show that the only problems in DPW lie with a few disgruntled employees and not the entire department. John DiMatteo, a worker whom the Wolfpack had attempted to coerce into joining their efforts, testified that he had never seen or heard about John Costello harassing any other employees. He went on to say that he never heard any of the DPW employees complain about Costello except for the four members of the Wolfpack. DiMatteo admitted that he had received memos from Costello for such infractions as driving his city too fast, and that he regarded such corrections not as harassment, but as Costello doing his job as supervisor. DiMatteo was quick to point out that he also had several memos from John, regarding a number of different assignments, praising what a good job he had done.

However, what really slammed the door in the face of the Wolfpack's allegations was the testimony of the man who had become their new boss. Ernie Purdy, who had since been elevated into the Director position, testified that as Costello's assistant, he had been in John's presence for roughly ninety-nine percent of the working day. Working together in such close proximity, Purdy asserted that he had frequent occasion to observe John's interactions with the many different personalities in the department, including the Wolfpack members. The new Director insisted that at no time had he ever observed his former boss harassing, intimidating or otherwise mistreating any DPW employee.

Unlike most of the previous defendants, former City Manager Tom Ciccarone proved to be quite adept at calmly jousting with attorneys. Having ironically fallen victim to the same "resign voluntarily or be terminated" edict with which he had bludgeoned Costello, Ciccarone had left Brigantine in April of 2000 only to land on his feet with another City Manager job in another small New Jersey town. Five months later, at his deposition, Chick saw a chance at redemption against the man he viewed as having precipitated his downfall. A true political operator, Ciccarone artfully claimed credit for most of the programs initiated by Costello and managed to apply an anti-Costello spin to almost any issue about which he was asked. For example, John had been praised for his efforts to reduce the incidents of Worker's Compensation abuse, which had been a serious problem in the department. Ciccarone, however, sought to discredit this accomplishment. It was his opinion that the poor workers were still being injured; they were just too frightened to file their claims now, for fear of being punished by Costello. Ciccarone has yet to explain the fact that under the apparently less frightening Ernie Purdy, a continuation of Costello's initiatives has resulted in similar results. Similarly, Ciccarone displayed a very convenient level of recollection at times, claiming even in the face of documentation to have no memory of Costello ever complaining to him about Councilman Frugoli interfering with DPW operation.

One big mystery was finally solved when, after thirteen months, Ciccarone finally revealed what he claimed was the "real" reason for demanding John's resignation. After refusing to disclose his rationale until under subpoena more than a year later, Ciccarone provided an anticlimax when he stated with a straight face that he had forced Costello out simply because their management styles were no longer compatible. Why it took over a year for Ciccarone to formulate that reason is a question to which the answer may never be known, but even taken at face value, Chick's reason does not hold up even when viewed alongside some of his other testimony. During the same deposition, Ciccarone also admitted that he had never once written any memo, nor otherwise documented in Costello's personnel file any criticism of his management style. Further refuting Ciccarone's claim of dissatisfaction with Costello was the testimony of two Brigantine City Council members, with whom Chick met frequently. Deputy Mayor Ed Kay testified that Ciccarone had never said anything to him that would indicate he was displeased with John's performance or style. Similarly, Councilman Sam Storino also maintained that Chick had never indicated any problem whatsoever with Costello. In fact, Storino went on to say that he would have been surprised had Ciccarone done so, what with the great job John had been doing.

In much the same spirit as the handwritten notes made by an illiterate man, Ciccarone also produced his own little piece of last minute, previously unmentioned evidence. To support his claims of Costello's unreasonable management style, Chick submitted a memo written by the City Clerk, Lois O'Connor, dated July 7, 1998, a week before the Manera killings. In the memo, supposedly written the morning after a council meeting at Ciccarone's behest, O'Connor seems to be swearing an affidavit. "*I personally recall that you mentioned to council that something had to be done to control John Costello or else you would have a mutiny on your hands.*" Why the City Manager would have felt it necessary to secure such documentation is a mystery, since any comments made during the meeting would have been recorded as part of the official minutes, a fact of which Ciccarone was well aware. Chick himself had no explanation as to why he would have requested such a memo be written at that particular time, since he had never done so before. When pressed, he smugly cited *"divine inspiration"* as the impetus behind his sudden decision to enlist his own personal witness. *"I asked her to write this. I didn't give her the words. This was the day after a Council meeting, in executive session. I don't recall the specifics of the conversation or the context of how it came up, but I did say something to the Mayor and Council and she has captured the essence of it here."*

Curiously, Deputy Mayor Ed "Scoop" Kay attended the meeting in question, and during his testimony adamantly denied that any such statement was made, asserting that Costello's name was not even mentioned during that meeting. Kay went on to disavow any knowledge of Ciccarone's memo, and repudiated any claim to its contents being part of the approved minutes of the City Council meeting. Councilman Sam Storino was also at the aforementioned meeting, and likewise had no recollection of any such statements regarding Costello. In fact, neither the Mayor nor any member of City Council testified that they had any knowledge whatsoever of Ciccarone's alleged remarks. Of course, the debate could have easily been settled with a quick review of the official minutes for the meeting in question. Unfortunately, closure on this issue, as well as the possible resultant perjury charge, was prevented by the city's refusal to release the tape of the meeting.

In further support for his decision to oust Costello, the cagey Ciccarone claimed to have conducted interviews with the DPW employees after the Manera killings. He even produced extensive, albeit undated, handwritten notes on these *"individual discussions with each member of the department"* that he claims to have undertaken at the request of the Mayor and City Council. In his effort to add credibility to his tale, Ciccarone even went so far as to list his procedure for the interviews. *"First, I wanted to know how they were doing, how they were coping with the trauma that everybody had been through with the Manera incident, to encourage them. Again, if they felt the need to talk to anybody that the psychologist was available for them. And then I told them I wanted to know from their perspective what had been going on down there and how they had been treated and how they saw other people being treated."* Despite such a formal-seeming process, none of the DPW employees deposed could recall any such meeting with Ciccarone or anyone else. Not even the members of the Wolfpack could be depended upon to confirm Chick's story. Neither Ken Miller nor Joe Lombardo testified that they were ever interviewed in such a manner, insisting that any conversations they had with Ciccarone were strictly of a casual nature. It almost seemed as if Ciccarone and the Wolfpack had gotten their signals crossed and had begun working at cross purposes; with Ciccarone seeking to justify his decision by virtue of eyewitness accounts, only to find himself hamstrung by the efforts of the Wolfpack members to avoid charges of collusion.

In one final attempt at damage control, Ciccarone claimed to have done an interview shortly after the killings with the Atlantic City Press, during which he'd been asked his opinion on whether or not he felt that John Costello was in any way responsible for Manera's actions. Summoning up his best impression of righteous indignation, Ciccarone recounted his reply. *"My response was that I thought that was ridiculous and that anybody that made that kind of suggestion is flat out wrong."* Of course, no evidence exists that this interview ever happened, because it was certainly not printed in the Atlantic City Press, or any other newspaper, for that matter. Like any good politician, Ciccarone refused to let the facts get in the way of a good story, offering up irrefutable evidence of his veracity. *"I know it was in the paper because Nick Manera had expressed to me many months or even a year later that his family was pissed off at me for it."* No copies of this mythical interview were ever produced. In truth, Ciccarone had never once issued any public statement to any media outlet, with regard to Costello and the misperceptions about his involvement in such a tragedy.

Ciccarone's lead supporter, Councilman James Frugoli, was no less duplicitous. Frugoli repeatedly changed his story to suit his purposes, contradicting himself several times over the course of his testimony. For example, in response to Costello's accusations that he had interfered with DPW operations, Frugoli categorically denied having circumvented the chain of command, claiming that he spent very little time at the DPW facility. *"I would stop in from time to time"* was his testimony.

In the face of a different charge, however, later in the same deposition that story changed. When pressed for evidence supporting his assertion that Costello had been too hard on the DPW employees, Frugoli found it convenient to characterize his visits to the Public Works facility much differently. Insisting that he had formed his opinion by having been present to witness examples of John's "rough" management style, now he claimed, *"I used to stop in and see John on a semi-daily basis."* However, even after changing his story, Frugoli still managed to contradict himself again, admitting that he had never actually witnessed Costello harassing or intimidating an employee. The Councilman could not even remember a specific instance where any employee had complained to him about Costello, but he still had the gall to continue to insist that John was too hard on his men.

Frugoli was not completely inept at the political game, however. Throughout his deposition, he demonstrated the cunning of a true politician by repeatedly taking advantage of the privilege provided by his city counsel seat. By law, Frugoli could not answer questions regarding any conversation or discussion that took place during an executive session of council. This provided him with a ready-made smokescreen to throw in the face of a determined questioner who refused to take *"I don't recall"* for an answer. Like the bulbous cephalopod he somewhat resembled, the Councilman would, in the face of any question that threatened to expose his lies and manipulations, eject a cloud of ink to confuse and mislead his pursuers long enough for him to dart away to safety. It began to seem as though Frugoli had been struck with a horribly selective memory ailment, one that rendered him almost completely unable to remember any conversations that were not protected by the executive session privilege.

The one council meeting Frugoli was willing to describe was one that, unfortunately, nobody else remembered. It was during this meeting, Frugoli contended, that Ciccarone had informed council of his intention to terminate John Costello's employment as head of DPW. Frugoli spun a tale of a righteously indignant Ciccarone refusing to elaborate on his reasons for this decision; instead warning the council that all they needed to know was that he wanted no interference on Costello's behalf. According to Frugoli, this display of conviction precluded any further inquiry by City Council as to the reason for Costello's potential termination. Predictably, no other City Council member testified that they had any recollection of such an exchange between Council and Ciccarone taking place at any time. Councilman Storino testified that he was completely unaware that Costello had even left DPW until almost a week after John had tendered his resignation, and that he suspected that he had been purposely left out of the loop to prevent any efforts on Costello's behalf.

However, Councilman Frugoli was not finished with his exhibition of misrepresentation and prevarication. He went on to claim that Costello had resigned voluntarily, and not while under duress. According to his logic, *"If Council had felt that way, we wouldn't have given him the severance package we did."* This so-called severance package was nothing more than Costello's unused accumulated vacation pay to which he was entitled in any event.

Frugoli proved the most intractable witness to be deposed in the case, mulishly refusing to concede even the most petty of details unless forced. He even disavowed his own political aspirations, perhaps for fear of tipping his hand too early. Long rumored to lust after the office of Mayor, Frugoli fiercely denied the suggestion during his testimony, despite having discussed his ambitions with Costello, who was after all the man in charge of the Republican Party in Brigantine, many times.

A new low was reached, however, when Frugoli went so far as to testify under oath that he had never even heard the expression "Outpost Four", the nickname with which he'd christened "his" ward. The Councilman's claim was somewhat discredited, however, when Costello produced a photograph of Frugoli's boat, a beautiful craft bearing the name "Outpost Four". Perhaps Frugoli should have named the boat during an executive session. Then at least he would have remembered it. He just would not have been able to talk about it.

Councilman Frugoli's boat, christened "Outpost Four" after the nickname for his ward he swore he'd never heard before.

As part of his persecution of Costello, Frugoli had been trying with all his political might to have John removed from the city's Zoning Board. Another member
of the committee told John that he had attended meetings of which the main
purpose had been to devise strategies to achieve just that end. The leading force
behind these meetings had been none other than Councilman James Frugoli,
who impartially pushed his own son John as Costello's replacement. During his
deposition, Frugoli claimed that he had only sought Costello's resignation from
the zoning board because of what he felt to be a conflict of interest caused by
John's present litigation against the city. However, in examining the dates, it
seems that Costello's reappointment to the Zoning Board, which Frugoli fought
so hard to prevent, occurred several months before the lawsuit against the city
was filed. After repeated attempts to oust Costello failed, Frugoli changed strategies and finally succeeded in achieving his aim of removing from his enemy all
possible avenues of power when he convinced the city to eliminate the Zoning
Board in its entirety.

Attempting to downplay the entire Zoning Board situation, Frugoli portrayed
such accusations of conspiratorial behavior as ridiculous. However, the testimony
of Deputy Mayor Ed Kay served to illustrate that what might seem ridiculous to a
normal person was just another day at the office in the Machiavellian world of

small town politics. When asked if Frugoli had ever approached him and inquired about the possibility of Kay persuading Costello to resign from the zoning board, Deputy Mayor Kay said, *"Outside of a meeting I can't discuss, I don't recall him saying that to me."* The meeting that Kay cannot discuss, at which Frugoli presumably *did* say that, would have been an executive session of council. Similarly, when asked if Frugoli had ever raised the subject of taking steps to see that Costello did not receive unemployment benefits, Deputy Mayor Kay replied, *"Not outside of executive session."* Once again, the obvious inference is that Frugoli did raise that topic in executive session.

Examined individually, the depositions of the witnesses reflected a wildly diverse range of intellectual and social proficiency, as well as several predictably varying perspectives on the same events. Taken as a whole, however, they formed a mosaic that presented a dire overall picture, that of some serious problems in the city of Brigantine. Whether or not a judge would ultimately decide that a city employee had been wrongly terminated had almost become a secondary issue in the eyes of Brigantine residents. Once the details of Costello's allegations were made public, many residents realized for the first time just how little knowledge they had concerning the activities of their so-called public servants. No matter the outcome of his litigation, John took comfort in the fact that the truth would finally be dragged out into the light of day for all to see.

14

Pucker Time at City Hall

With all the evidence presented and all the witnesses deposed, the case was ready to proceed to the next stage. Assigned to the case was federal judge Jerome B Simandle, whose main duty at this stage was to examine the evidence and testimony in order to review the merits of each individual charge and decide which, if any, would be sent to trial. Simandle's first task was to render decisions on the myriad of motions filed by all three groups of defendants.

The first official legal maneuvering began when all three sets of defendants filed separate motions to have the case dismissed, known as a request for summary judgment. In any court case, once the plaintiff or prosecutor has made his charges and presented his supporting evidence, the defendant will usually file a blanket motion to dismiss for failure to state a claim upon which relief can be granted. This does not actually attack the merits of the case, but merely tests the legal sufficiency of the complaint. A standard tactic that rarely works, a motion for summary judgment is nevertheless always worth a shot. Unfortunately for a defendant hoping to get lucky, the standard for granting a summary judgment is a stringent one. A court may grant summary judgment only when the materials of record show that there is no genuine issue as to material fact and that the party making t0 he motion is entitled to judgment as a matter of law.

When considering such a general motion to dismiss, the reviewing court must accept as true all allegations in the complaint and view them in the light most favorable to the plaintiff. The court must also accept as true any reasonable inferences derived from these facts. Finally, the court may not dismiss the complaint unless it appears beyond all doubt that the plaintiff can prove no set of facts in support of his claim. The question therefore before the court is not whether the plaintiff will ultimately prevail; rather it is whether they can prove any of their claims in a trial. Upon review of the case, Simandle ruled that evidence to support many of Costello's allegations did indeed exist. As a result, the general motion to dismiss was denied.

Expecting such an outcome, all three sets of defendants had more specific dismissal motions already prepared. The City Defendants filed for dismissal on the grounds that John's suit had not been filed within the required time limit. According to the New Jersey Tort Claims Act, an individual wishing to file a lawsuit must do so within ninety days of the adverse employment action that precipitated the litigation. The defendants took the position that since ninety-six days had elapsed between the day Ciccarone first demanded Costello's resignation and the filing of the suit, the case should be dismissed. The plaintiff's position was that since he had continued working after receiving the ultimatum from Ciccarone, the ninety days time limit did not begin until the day he actually handed in his resignation, which was only eighty-nine days before he filed his lawsuit. Judge Simandle ruled that Costello's state of mind showed that he still felt that his job could be saved until the day he resigned, since Ciccarone had left it up to him to decide whether to resign or not. John had never been given a specific date at which his employment would end. Instead, he had continued to attend work and spent the week following Ciccarone's ultimatum in communication with city officials in an attempt to save his job. Therefore, the motion to dismiss the case for exceeding the allotted time limit was denied.

Another motion to dismiss was filed by the Media Defendants, who claimed that John Costello had become a public figure, and as such, was not entitled to as much protection from defamation as a private individual. New Jersey law takes an expansive view of the types of government employees who may be considered public officials. Upon review of the facts, Simandle pointed out that Costello had brought public acclaim upon himself and the DPW because of the changes he'd made, and that he had considered himself an agent of the public's welfare when he pointed out the water problems. Considering also the fact that John was Municipal Chairman of the Republican Club and head of the Zoning Board, Simandle said, *"Both his political activism and his voluntary membership on an important regulatory body demonstrate that Costello consistently sought out high-profile public positions. Based on this fact, as well as the uncontested evidence of the public's deep interest in the workings of the DPW, and the public's interest in Costello's performance as DPW Director, the court finds as a matter of law that Costello was a public figure."*

The legal standards for proving defamation against a media outlet are much more demanding for public officials and public figures, so as a result of this ruling, it was decided that Costello was not entitled to the same level of protection as a private citizen. A private individual may succeed in a defamation suit simply by demonstrating negligence, which could certainly have been proven against TV40. However, those designated as public officials must go beyond negligence and prove actual malice. Especially in a matter of public concern, the media is afforded much more protection against charges of defamation. To satisfy the actual malice standard, Costello had to show by clear and convincing evidence that the defendants either knew the broadcast statements were false, or published the statements with a reckless disregard for the truth. Mere evidence of negligent publishing or failure to fully investigate the story does not suffice. In his decision, Judge Simandle acknowledged the possibility of malice, but went on to state that a mere possibility is not enough. *"The plaintiff's claims against the Media include some evidence from which a reasonable jury could infer actual malice, but not the clear and convincing evidence needed to survive summary judgment."*

Therefore, the defamation charges against the Media Defendants were dismissed. Since they hinged on the defamation charges, the charge of intentional infliction of emotional distress against TV40 was dismissed as well. However, Simandle did not dismiss the charges without offering this criticism of the journalistic practices of the Media Defendants. *"The record here demonstrates that Reporter Silver had knowledge of the inconsistencies and unreliability of the Manera/Costello story, but nevertheless proceeded to broadcast untrue statements about Costello's role in the tragedy. It is true that Silver could have, and probably should have, done more to investigate the Costello/Manera story, and should have presented a more balanced report to the public."*

Also dismissed were the charges of defamation leveled against Ciccarone, Frugoli and the City of Brigantine itself. Simandle decided that although Ciccarone may have neglected his duty as City Manager by allowing the DPW employees to make public accusations against a city official with no clarification of the city's official position, he had not personally uttered any of the defamatory statements himself. Nor had Frugoli, or any other official representative of the city, for that matter. In fact, the televised vilification of Costello had been met with a deafening silence by the officials of Brigantine and allowed to stand as the only public comment on the issue, a fact that was not lost on Judge Simandle. *"While plaintiffs have not alleged that Ciccarone and Frugoli directly made statements causing plaintiff emotional distress, they have alleged concert of action between these defendants and the Union defendants who actually spread the falsehoods about Costello."* While he allowed for the possibility of such a conspiracy, Simandle ruled that the charges of defamation, as such, did not apply against these defendants. The judge also explained that the city itself could not be held accountable for the comments of Gibson, Hopkins, Miller and Lombardo, because there was no indication that they were acting within the scope of their employment when they made their defamatory remarks.

However, the defamation charges against the individual Wolfpack members and the Teamsters' union, known collectively as the Union defendants, were firmly upheld. The judge immediately set the tone of his remarks regarding the Wolfpack when he started by plainly stating what seemed to be the very essence of the case. *"The plaintiffs suggest that Lombardo and Gibson developed the plan to falsely blame Costello for the Manera incident on the day of the murder/suicide. There is evidence to support this theory."* In explaining his decision to uphold the defamation charges, Simandle demonstrated a complete mastery of the facts of the case and a clear focus on the evidence elicited in the depositions. *"The question with respect to the statements made by Miller, Gibson, Lombardo and Tucker concerning Costello's alleged role in causing Manera's violent crime is whether there is clear and convincing evidence that their statements were knowingly false."* The answer to that question was found in an examination of the testimony given by John's assistant and eventual replacement, Ernie Purdy. Simandle went on to compare Purdy's statement to those of the Wolfpack members and the Teamsters' officials. *"In contrast to the Union defendants' statements concerning Costello's "harassment" of Manera and other DPW workers, Purdy, who testified that he was with Costello 75% of the working day, and throughout the 3½ years Costello oversaw the DPW, stated under oath that he never saw Costello harass or physically threaten any DPW employees. There is probative evidence that Costello had not singled Manera out for unfair treatment at the DPW, and that, despite their public proclamations that Costello was to blame, the Wolfpack was aware that the event that precipitated Manera's conduct was his wife's decision to leave him. Based on the foregoing, a reasonable jury would be justified in finding by clear and convincing evidence that the Wolfpack and Union defendants acted with knowing falsity when they publicly blamed Costello for Manera's murder/suicide."*

Also upheld was Costello's claim that his civil rights had been violated when he had been forced to resign from his position. The law states that government officials may not take adverse employment action against an individual in retaliation for exercise of that individual's First Amendment rights. However, in order for speech by a government employee to be protected, it must relate to a matter of public concern, a point that was hotly disputed by the defense attorneys, to no avail. Judge Simandle found that John had indeed engaged in protected activity when he spoke out against Frugoli's shenanigans and the Wolfpack's activities to the City Manager. The fact that no action was taken to address or even investigate Costello's complaints, and instead, John himself was thereafter subjected to further mistreatment, went far to support the plaintiff's claim of First Amendment retaliation.

As grounds to challenge Costello's claim of intentional infliction of emotional distress (IIED), the defendants argued that the complaint had not alleged conduct sufficiently outrageous to state a valid case of IIED. To establish a claim for IIED, plaintiff must prove the following: (1) That defendant engaged in conduct that was so extreme and outrageous as to go beyond all possible bounds of decency, and to be regarded as atrocious and utterly intolerable in a civilized community; and (2) the conduct was intended to produce the emotional distress, or was in deliberate disregard of a high probability that emotional distress will follow; and (3) the plaintiff suffered emotional distress so severe that no reasonable person could be expected to endure it; and finally, that (4) the defendant's actions were the proximate cause of the plaintiff's emotional distress. Upon applying these four requirements to the claims made by Costello, Simandle found that John had more than met the standard. *"The Court agrees with the plaintiff that this is no simple case where an employee suffers some mental stress on account of his firing. Rather, the defendant's behavior was designed to force Costello from his job at the expense of his reputation and community standing. If it is proven that the defendants attempted to attach Costello's name to the Manera incident simply to further their efforts to remove Costello as head of the DPW, then the defendants certainly will have been shown to have engaged in conduct that exceeds all possible bounds of decency."*

Costello's charge of malicious interference with prospective economic advantage was next on the block. The defendants were being accused of interfering with John's contract and causing him to lose a job that he had all expectation of keeping. In this case, the only arguable issue involved City Manager Tom Ciccarone, since he was the only defendant with any business at all being involved in Costello's termination. Ciccarone protested that since he was Costello's boss, he had every right to fire John, so therefore, cannot be accused of interfering with a contract he had the right to terminate.

In his decision, Judge Simandle addressed this point. *"Based on the evidence of concert of action between the Union defendants, Frugoli and Ciccarone to oust Costello from his position as Director, the Court finds that this claim may go forward. Ciccarone, however argues that he was acting pursuant to his job as City Manager when he terminated Costello, and thus cannot be held liable for interfering with a business relationship with which he was directly involved. Plaintiffs claim that Ciccarone was acting with malice when he terminated Costello, and thus was acting outside the scope of his employment. Ciccarone, as City Manager was in a position to stop the Union defendants from undermining Costello's efforts. Not only did he fail to take remedial action, but he allied himself with Frugoli and the Union defendants, and failed to counter the outrageous statements being made in the press about Costello's link to the Manera incident. The Court finds that evidence in this case is sufficient to create a triable issue that Ciccarone acted with malice."*

The charge of abuse of process against the Union defendants was next to be attacked. In this instance, Costello was charging that the Wolfpack members, with support from the Teamsters' officials, abused the grievance process by filing frivolous complaints, in order to further their agenda rather than to complain about actual harassment. In support of this argument, Costello pointed out that not a single charge or grievance filed against him was ever resolved in the filer's favor. All the grievances filed in connection with Costello's job assignments were dismissed without action, and the unfair labor practice charge filed with the Public Employment Relations Commission (PERC) was dismissed for vagueness. Furthermore, the Wolfpack openly advised Ciccarone that their strategy was to continuously file grievances against Costello in an effort to undermine his support and in furtherance of their aim to have him removed as Director. Simandle went on to say, *"The Court finds that plaintiffs have presented sufficient evidence of malice in connection with the defendants' grievance and complaint filings that the abuse of process claim may proceed to trial."*

The most complicated and potentially damaging charge for the defendants was addressed last. Costello's charge that the defendants had violated the Conscientious Employee Protection Act (CEPA), brought with it heavy penalties if proven. Also known as the Whistleblower Law, CEPA protects employees who "blow the whistle" on illegal or improper activities in the workplace from being retaliated against by their employers. CEPA claims are very complicated because of the fact that the burden of proof switches back and forth throughout the process. First, the plaintiff must make out a prima facie case of retaliatory discharge. This initial burden requires that the plaintiff show that: (1) he reasonably believed illegal conduct was occurring; (2) he either (a) disclosed or threatened to disclose the activity to a supervisory or public body or (b) objected to or refused to participate in the illegal conduct. The plaintiff must then also show that (3) retaliatory action was taken against him; and that (4) there was a causal connection between the whistle blowing and the adverse employment action.

Once the plaintiff has established his case, the burden of production then shifts to the defendant to articulate some legitimate, non-retaliatory reason for its actions. Once the defendant gives what he claims to be his legitimate reason for the adverse action, the burden then shifts back to the plaintiff once again to show that the proffered reason for discharge was a lie.

It is then up to the court to determine whether the plaintiff has offered sufficient evidence for a reasonable jury to find that the defendant's proffered reason for discharge was false and that retaliation for the whistle blowing was the actual reason behind the adverse employment action. Typically, the types of evidence offered by the plaintiff at this stage are inconsistencies or anomalies that could support an inference that the employer did not act for its stated reasons.

After a careful review of the facts of the case, Judge Simandle determined that Costello had created a triable issue that he had engaged in activity protected by CEPA, and therefore deserved protection under the law. In fact, Simandle found more than one instance in which the law may have been violated. ""*The record includes evidence of at least two types of activity that Costello could have considered illegal conduct, and which he tried to prevent or refused to participate in. First, Costello instituted many remedial changes at DPW, including worker's compensation abuse and theft of the city's water services.*"

"*Because Costello's efforts had an impact on the cleanliness of the island's water supply, which is a factor touching upon public health concerns, a reasonable jury might find that Costello's efforts at exposing the abuses within the DPW was protected activity under the CEPA law.*"

"The record contains strong evidence that Costello refused to accede to unlawful requests by Councilman Frugoli. The court finds that a reasonable person in Costello's position could certainly have felt that the dumping of dirt behind Coquille Beach development was unlawful and dangerous to the environment. Costello's rejection of Frugoli's repeated requests to raise the pathway could certainly be seen by a reasonable jury as an objection to or refusal to engage in activity that would have been harmful to the environment, and therefore, Costello's conduct in this respect might reasonably be found protectable under (the CEPA law)."

However, because of the details of this particular situation, Costello was faced with an even heavier burden of proof than might have normally been the case. Only retaliation by an employer is prohibited by CEPA. Of all the defendants, only Ciccarone had the power to terminate Costello. In other words, to succeed at trial in showing that Costello was fired because the Teamsters' union, the Wolfpack members and Councilman Frugoli wanted him fired, John had to prove that Ciccarone was adopting or ratifying the Union defendants' and Frugoli's unlawful motives. Thus, the question became whether Ciccarone (1) knew of the illegal acts of the Wolfpack, Union and Frugoli, (2) knew of John's refusal to allow or participate in these unlawful acts, and (3) terminated Costello's employment because of his will to allow the illegal acts to continue or to punish Costello for failing to participate in or condone those acts.

Addressing this issue, Simandle said, *"Ciccarone had extensive knowledge of the efforts of some DPW employees to disrupt Costello's attempts to reform the DPW. Ciccarone was also aware of the Wolfpack's scheme to get rid of Costello, as well as Costello's opposition to their conduct. There is also evidence that Ciccarone was fully aware of Frugoli's repeated and improper requests for special treatment from Costello. In light of the foregoing, the Court finds that there is evidence from which a reasonable jury could find that Ciccarone adopted or ratified the unlawful motives of the Wolfpack, Union and Frugoli when he terminated Costello's employment. Ciccarone had clear notice from the Union and Wolfpack that they intended to undermine Costello's authority, and did nothing. Ciccarone also made it understood that Costello should not refuse Frugoli's demands.*

The next phase of CEPA is for the city to state its reason for discharge. Ciccarone had testified at his deposition that he decided to terminate Costello after interviewing DPW employees after the Manera incident and concluding that John's management style was too harsh and had created a hostile work environment at the DPW. Judge Simandle remarked, *"This contrasts with Ciccarone's explanation to Costello for his firing, which was no explanation at all."*

While it is true that Ciccarone did not and was not required to give a reason for his decision to terminate Costello, the fact that he publicly offered reasons for his decision once challenged with accusations of retaliatory discharge means that Ciccarone's motives are now subject to scrutiny for evidence of pretext. Simandle said, *"The present record contains inconsistencies and anomalies that cast doubt on Ciccarone's proffered legitimate reasons for discharge. While Ciccarone now states that Costello's rough managerial tactics motivated his decision to fire him, there is ample evidence that Ciccarone actually appreciated Costello's performance."*

Simandle made reference to the budget proposal that Ciccarone had made to city council in which the City Manager had praised Costello as having made the DPW *"More efficient and accountable than it has ever been"* and praised the *"team effort which is making the department successful."* Simandle pointed out, *"It is significant that the budget statement speaks of a team effort between Costello and the employees of DPW. Obviously, this public statement of support for Mr. Costello, and the manner in which he, his subordinates, DPW employees, and the Teamsters Union were working together contrasts with Ciccarone's statement during the course of this litigation that he fired Costello because of heavy-handed management tactics."*

In the end, Simandle determined that Costello had successfully demonstrated pretext, which allowed the CEPA case to survive summary judgment and go to trial. Simandle reasons, *"The contrast between Ciccarone's past and present assessments of Costello's performance is evidence from which a reasonable jury could disbelieve the defendant's proferred reason for discharge. Based on the inconsistencies of record regarding Ciccarone's consistently favorable evaluations of Costello's performance at the time, and his later-articulated opinion-stated only after the commencement of this litigation—that Costello was creating a hostile work environment, a reasonable fact finder would be justified in disbelieving Ciccarone's proferred reasons for discharge, and drawing an inference of pretext."*

When the smoke cleared, the majority of the charges leveled at the defendants by Costello survived summary judgment and were continued on to trial. While the Media defendants had escaped the litigation, the city and union defendants found themselves even more hopelessly entangled in a web of their own creation. Now that it had been determined that the suit would proceed to trial, the mad scramble began to not only avoid a costly litigation, but also to prevent the public airing of the little island's dirty laundry.

15

Taxpayers Lose Again

Once it became apparent that the case would indeed be going to trial, and that all of the allegations made by Costello would become part of the public record, the efforts of Brigantine's attorneys immediately moved from contesting the facts to getting the case settled quietly. No longer were any of the defendants interested in denying their culpability. The focus was now squarely on how best to suppress the details of Costello's case and avoid the public relations disaster that would surely result from their disclosure, not to mention possible criminal charges stemming from some of the more serious allegations.

For his part, John recognized the wisdom of negotiating a settlement, but at the same time, a part of him wanted nothing more than to have his day in court and drag all the island's dirty little secrets out into the light. That attitude led Costello to turn down several offers of settlement, much to the chagrin of his attorney, Greg Saputelli, who felt compelled to explain some of the facts of legal life to his client. The realities of the justice system in America are such that most litigants are encouraged to avoid forcing their case to trial. Judges have a vested interest in settling cases before trial and saving the time and money a trial would cost, especially at the Federal level. A plaintiff who rejects what is to the judge's eye a reasonable settlement and that insists on going to court can find himself facing an uphill battle on unfriendly terrain. Under such circumstances, said plaintiff risks walking away empty-handed, or with so minimal an award as to make the rejected settlement offer seems generous by comparison. This possibility was even more strongly stressed by the already impatient judge once Costello insisted that his attorney turn down an offer of one million dollars to settle the case.

John's decision, which raised eyebrows even among his own legal team, was based on the inclusion of the Wolfpack members in the settlement agreement. The city was caught on the horns of a dilemma concerning the Wolfpack members. As desirable as it may have been to exclude them from the settlement offer, under the terms of their contracts the city was forced to include them. Brigantine could have faced additional litigation from each of the four Wolfpack members, who would have certainly expected the city to pay their costs, plus whatever damages Costello may have been awarded at their expense. Rather than face the unknowable costs involved under such circumstances, it was far easier to bring the Wolfpack members under the umbrella. However, John was not prepared to allow his four main antagonists off the hook without extracting an additional pound of flesh. If the city insisted that the four troublemakers be included in the settlement, Costello demanded that he receive what he referred to as, *"an extra fifty thou per bonehead."* The city's insurance carrier, already approaching the limit of their coverage, quickly acquiesced. On December 20, John settled his suit against the City of Brigantine and its employees for a total payment of $1.2 million. The city itself would be liable only for a $25,000 deductible, with the balance paid by its insurer, the Municipal Excess Liability Joint Insurance Fund. However, the city could have been forced to pay much more had Costello won at trial. As a condition of the agreement, Costello had to promise not to use his newly won war chest to run for political office in Brigantine. He also had to agree to step down as head of the Zoning Board, although City Council had already abolished the board a month prior, in an effort to reduce John's influence and public presence. Although there was no gag order in effect regarding the terms of the settlement, the amount paid to Costello by the city was a closely guarded secret and was not disclosed to the public until an Atlantic City newspaper invoked the Right-To-Know Law to obtain the terms and published them on January 4.

In the meantime, Costello's suit against the Teamsters' union and its officers was still scheduled for trial. After extensive negotiations between the two sides, John reached a settlement agreement with the Teamsters' defendants, the terms of which may not be disclosed because of a gag order requested by the defendants. However, Costello did receive a retraction letter from the union disclaiming the accusations leveled at him during and after his employment with the DPW.

Joseph Yeoman
President/Executive Officer

FEB 22 2002

~~January 17, 2002~~

Mr. And Mrs. John Costello
518 Caverly Drive
Brigantine, NJ 08203

Dear Mr. And Mrs. Costello:

This will confirm that both you and Chauffeurs, Teamsters, Helpers Local Union No. 331, Joseph Yeoman and David Tucker, have agreed to resolve the matters in dispute between them in the case captioned <u>John T. Costello, et al. v. City of Brigantine, et Als.</u> Civil Action No. 99cv4072 (JBS).

This will further confirm that Local Union 331 does not believe that John Costello had any causal effect, direct or indirect, in the murder/suicide of Joseph Manera and his wife, and hereby retracts any implication to the contrary.

Furthermore, Local Union 331 does not believe that Mr. Costello had any culpability with respect to the grievances and municipal court harassment complaints field against him while he was Director of the Brigantine Department of Public works.

Sincerely,

Joseph Yeoman
Joseph Yeoman
President & Executive Officer

/ch

As part of the settlement agreement, Teamsters' local 331 was required to furnish John Costello with this letter, denouncing all the false accusations leveled against him.

Throughout the city of Brigantine, the reaction to the settlement varied, depending on the perspective of the observer. Most residents who were aware of the situation had supported Costello from the beginning, but would rather have had him reinstated than see the city forced to pay out over a million dollars to mollify him. Of course, friends of relatives of the defendants all felt that an injustice had taken place. The Brigantine Taxpayer's Association demanded an accounting of city's lawyer bills, but that demand was ignored. To prevent this information from reaching the public, the City Council held a secret meeting and declared the attorneys' billing records to be "privileged" information and not a matter of public record. Residents were permitted to pay for everything with their taxes, but were not permitted to see the price tag. In truth, the city paid its attorney, who actually slept through many of the depositions, over $75,000. Many residents are also still interested in the allegations leveled in the suit by Costello. Tina Chaplin, President of the Brigantine Taxpayer's Association, wrote a letter to a Brigantine newspaper, asking, *"What is the status of the lawsuit brought by John & Barbara Costello against the City of Brigantine? A lot of serious charges have been raised in this action, charges that need to be aired and addressed in a public forum so the taxpayers of Brigantine know the truth."*

In their first public comments on the case, Mayor Phil Guenther and City Council attempted to explain why they had authorized paying the settlement, while at the same time still insisting that Costello's allegations of corruption were not true. Former council member Anne Phillips, representing the Brigantine Taxpayer's Association, questioned the officials during the public portion of the council meeting, but never could seem to obtain a straight answer. At first, Council members insisted that they could not comment on the case because of a confidentiality provision in the settlement. However, as Phillips continued to question them, several grew visibly agitated and engaged in a sometimes-heated exchange with her. *"We regret that this lawsuit didn't go to trial where all the charges could have been aired and a jury verdict rendered, assigning blame for any wrongdoing,"* Phillips said. She wondered aloud why, if they did not believe Costello's allegations were true, did the city officials authorize payment of the largest settlement of a suit of this type in the history of the state.

Mayor Guenther said that the city's insurance carrier had recommended settling the case. He said that if City Council did not agree with their recommendation, the city would have been held liable for any additional money over the $1.2 million proposed settlement if the case went to trial and Costello won. The mayor said that by settling, council insured that the city would not have to pay more than the minimum deductible of $25,000. *"We have a fiduciary responsibility to the taxpayers,"* Guenther said, somehow keeping a straight face. However, it was subsequently revealed that the amount paid out by the city itself was actually more than $100,000, when payments made to city prosecutor William Gasbarro, for serving as liaison between the city and its insurance carrier, were factored in. When confronted with this discrepancy, Guenther did a fast two-step and insisted that he had only been asked previously how much of the *settlement* Brigantine had been forced to pay, not their total expenses. Since those legal fees were not part of the settlement, Guenther innocently insisted, city officials had seen no reason to mention them when discussing the settlement.

Councilman Richard Cassamento, even more tenuously connected to the world of reality, went on to claim that, *"Many of us would have liked to have seen this darn thing go to trial."* Casamento actually claimed that Council was concerned that the September 11, 2001 terrorist attacks could have created sympathy for Costello and resulted in a jury verdict against the city, based on emotion. Casamento's point was less than clear to many in the audience, and he was lambasted in a subsequent editorial in the Press of Atlantic City for these claims.

As for the allegations of misconduct and corruption leveled against the city during the suit, the mayor and council said that they saw no evidence of any truth to Costello's allegations. Nor did they see any need to investigate the claims. Anne Phillips was accused of political motivations when she insisted on questioning council further on the allegations, when they were obviously ready to put the matter behind them. She asked the city officials if they had taken any steps to prevent the DPW from returning to what she called *"pre-Costello conditions."* Mayor Guenther bristled at the suggestion and defiantly suggested that if Phillips or anyone else had evidence of corruption, they should forward it to the Atlantic County Prosecutor's Office. He refused to discuss the matter any further and forbid any council members from responding to Phillips' questions regarding the allegations. An editorial in the Atlantic City Press offered advice to the Brigantine Mayor and City Council. *"Folks, you settled a whistle-blower lawsuit from former Public Works Director John Costello for the whopping amount of $1.2 million. That's not chump change. If your insurance carrier thought you ought to settle for that amount, sounds like the carrier wasn't too confident you'd win the case."* The editorial closed with the following admonition, *"So, elected officials of Brigantine, please don't be surprised if some members of the public ask whether the situation has been corrected. Don't get defensive when they ask what controls are in place to ensure the department functions efficiently. Don't deflect the questions by accusing the people ask-*

ing them of being politically motivated. They are perfectly reasonable questions, given the circumstances. Just answer them."

Ironically, instead of exposing the hidden web of corruption and deceit throughout Brigantine's government, the settlement of the Costello case only served to bolster the resolve of the city's officials to close ranks and observe the code of silence imposed by the ruling elite. While John's first priority was certainly to redress the specific wrongs done him by the defendants in the case and to repair his damaged reputation, he had also hoped to serve the residents of his hometown one last time. Brigantine's residents have been kept in the dark for far too long about the abuses that had been perpetrated in their name by those who had been given, and who had betrayed, the public trust. Many of the problems in Brigantine will seem all too familiar to many residents of other towns; towns with their own ruling elite, their own shadow government, their own inner circle. To be sure, Brigantine is not the only town where such conditions exist, but Brigantine is certainly an example of such a town.

Expressing the sentiments of many of the island's inhabitants, one resident wrote a letter to a Brigantine paper, lamenting the loss of what he had seen as a true public servant. His letter captured the spirit of John Costello's perspective on his task as Director of Public Works.

"While I waited to speak with Mr. Costello, I noticed a statement by him that was framed and hanging on the wall in his office. His statement summed up all the observations I had made and should, by the way, be adopted and govern all of Brigantine's other public departments. That statement follows:

'The Public Works Mission Statement

Brigantine residents are the most important people to enter this office, in person, by mail, or by telephone. Brigantine residents are not dependent on us. On the contrary, we are dependent on them. Brigantine residents are not an interruption of our work, they are the purpose of it. Our work begins and ends with the residents of Brigantine, and is measured by how well we serve them.'"

Epilogue

In the wake of the settlement, not much has changed in the small island community of Brigantine. Some of the players have changed positions, or been carried off the field, but, as is usually the case in the world of small town politics, the game goes on.

Tom Ciccarone left his job with the city of Brigantine shortly following the settlement of the case. Ironically, Chick was forced out under the same "resign or be terminated" conditions he had forced on John Costello, with expensive results. He now serves as City Manager of Chatham Township, an affluent North Jersey suburb. The city's legal firm, based in nearby Florham Park, NJ, was instrumental in helping Ciccarone secure his new position. At his retirement party, which was held at the DPW facility, Emmitt Turner, former political maven and owner of the Brigantine Times, attended with his camera. He snapped a photo of Miller, Hopkins, and Lombardo and captioned the photo by referring to the group as "The Wolfpack."

Ernie Purdy continues to serve as DPW director. After taking over for Costello, he has held the post to this date. He now stands as the fourth highest paid municipal employee in the city, drawing an annual salary of $72,500.

The Coquille Beach path is now a nice wide road, regardless of the wetlands situation. Immediately after Costello was deposed and Purdy took over his job, the path was indeed filled in and widened, drastically expanding its dimensions. What was once a small path is now a dirt road raised 3 feet in elevation and widened to 16 feet, containing all the asphalt and sewer line shards and materials that Doran stated should not be on the beach. Nobody contacted the DEP about the wetlands issue. The proposed improvement was not presented to the public. The final job was never inspected. To this day, nobody is sure, whether the Coquille Beach condominium residents got a freebie at City expense, or if the city violated the wetlands laws. Furthermore, nobody seems to care. In the end, Councilman Frugoli got his road, and his votes. Later, in his deposition for the case, he simply denied everything. He denied that Costello had told him they could not build the road. He denied that the area in question qualified as wetlands. He even denied talking about it with Doran, even though Doran testified he had. When Doran's testimony was read to him, Frugoli claimed he could not recall that conversation.

Teamsters local 331 was featured in the NLPC's (National Legal and Policy Center) Organized Labor Accountability Project 2/4/2000 "Union Corruption Update" which advertises itself as "Information on America's most corrupt and aggressive unions." Union Corruption Update is part of NLPC's Organized Labor Accountability Project, which is investigating and exposing corruption in the Teamsters, LIUNA, AFL-CIO and many other union organizations. NLPC is a nonpartisan, nonprofit foundation promoting ethics and accountability in government through research, education and legal action. David Tucker no longer serves as Business Agent for local 331.

The Wolfpack is still employed by the Brigantine DPW. It is not hard to imagine the faction running roughshod over their new boss, now that they've shown what they could do to the last guy who tried to make them work. Ken Miller has returned to being chauffeured to and from work, because of yet another DWI conviction. This time, he will need to be picked up and dropped off every day for two years.

James Frugoli is still the representative for Outpost Four, also known as Brigantine's Fourth ward. There are now three generations of Frugolis occupying spots on the city payroll. Not only have the Councilman and both his sons jumped on board the municipal gravy train, but now his grandson has as well.

Ed "Scoop" Kay, disgusted and dismayed, retired from Brigantine's political scene.

Sam Storino, Richard Casamento, Robert Solari and Sue Schilling still serve on the Brigantine City Council. Phil Guenther still serves as Mayor. Sue Schilling, in addition to her duties for the city, also serves as moral conscience for the county, as a Freeholder.

City Council has refused to reveal the total billing from the attorneys on the case to the Brigantine Taxpayer's Association. They also refuse to reveal the minutes from the meeting during which Ciccarone claims to have warned them about the impending danger of John Costello's management style.

All municipal office holders in Brigantine successfully ran for re-election in November of 2004. All candidates were unopposed. Obviously, whatever the cost of the settlement to the taxpayers, it was worth it to them.

The Costellos have moved out of Brigantine and are enjoying retirement and the company of their grandchildren.

Cast of Characters

BRIGANTINE CITY OFFICIALS

Phillip Guenther....Mayor of Brigantine
Ed "Scoop" Kay....Deputy Mayor
Sue Schilling....Councilperson at Large
Robert Solari....First Ward Councilman
Richard Casamento....Second Ward Councilman
Salvatore "Sam" Storino....Third Ward Councilman
Anne Phillips....former Third Ward Councilperson
James Frugoli....Fourth Ward Councilman
Thomas Ciccarone....City Manager
Matt Doran....City Engineer
Lois O'Connor....City Clerk
James Barber....Director of Public Safety
Matthew Giacobbe....Attorney for City Defendants
William Gasbarro....Attorney for City Defendants
Peter Tucci....Attorney for City Defendants

DPW EMPLOYEES

John Costello....Director of Department of Public Works
Ernie Purdy....Assistant Director
Robert Gibson Sr.....Former Superintendent of Public Works, father of Bobby*
Mike Hopkins....DPW Employee, Wolfpack member, DPW shop steward*
Bobby Gibson....DPW Employee, Wolfpack member*
Ken Miller....DPW Employee, Wolfpack member*
Joe Lombardo....DPW Employee, Wolfpack member*
Joseph Manera....DPW Employee

Nick Manera....DPW Employee
Carmen Danunzio....DPW Employee, Supervisor of Water & Sewer Dept.*
John DiMatteo....DPW Employee
Kelly Wilson....DPW Receptionist*

UNION OFFICIALS

Joseph Yeoman....Business Manager/CEO, Teamsters' local 331
David Tucker....Business Agent, Teamsters' local 331
Peter Marks....Attorney for Union defendants

MEDIA DEFENDANTS

Lisa Johnson....News anchor, TV40 news
Kara Silver...On-air reporter, TV40 news
Jack Gorny....Attorney for Media Defendants

PROFESSIONALS

Gregory Saputelli, Esq....Lead Attorney for Plaintiff
Eric G. Filkry....Associate attorney
Christine A. Campbell....Associate attorney
William Taggart....Plaintiff's private investigator
Dr. Edward Black....Plaintiff's forensic psychiatrist
Bunin Associates...Actuarial economic consulants
Schlesinger Associates....Plaintiff's trial consultant
U.S. District Court Judge Jerome Simandle...Presiding judge for case

About the Author

Patrick Costello was raised on the island of Brigantine and was a DPW summer-employee. He felt himself uniquely qualified to chronicle his father's adventures in small town politics. This is his first book, but Patrick has previously contributed to such publications as the *Press of Atlantic City* and the *Philadelphia Daily News*, as well as several top online periodicals. Patrick is currently working on his next book project.

978-0-595-36763-4
0-595-36763-1